T0277413

True Companions
Life in the field and home with our hunting dogs

True Companions
Life in the field and home with our hunting dogs

Chris Madson

STACKPOLE
BOOKS
Essex, Connecticut
Blue Ridge Summit, Pennsylvania

STACKPOLE BOOKS
An imprint of Globe Pequot, the trade division of
The Rowman & Littlefield Publishing Group, Inc.
4501 Forbes Blvd., Ste. 200
Lanham, MD 20706
www.rowman.com

Distributed by NATIONAL BOOK NETWORK

Copyright © 2023 by Chris Madson

All rights reserved. No part of this book may be reproduced in any
form or by any electronic or mechanical means, including information
storage and retrieval systems, without written permission from the
publisher, except by a reviewer who may quote passages in a review.

British Library Cataloguing in Publication Information available

Library of Congress Cataloging-in-Publication available

ISBN 978-0-8117-7353-9 (cloth : alk. paper)
ISBN 978-0-8117-7354-6 (epub)

∞™ The paper used in this publication meets the minimum
requirements of American National Standard for Information
Sciences—Permanence of Paper for Printed Library Materials,
ANSI/NISO Z39.48-1992.

Versions of some of these essays have appeared in other publications:
Sporting Classics magazine: "The Twenty-One" (2016), "Judy's
Cranberry Chocolate Chip Bread" (2018), and "The Bell" (2012).
Pheasants Forever magazine: "Zen in the Art of Wingshooting" (2019),
"Bet Your Boots" (2020), and "A Hard School" (2022). *Wing & Shot*
magazine: "Pointing the Way" (2001) and "What's Worth Saving"
(1999). *Arizona Wildlife Views* magazine: "Discovering the Desert"
(2016). *Covey Rise*: "The Rainbow" (2021). *North American Grouse*
magazine: "A Few Points on Prairie Grouse" (2021) and "Fool's Hens"
(2021). Thanks to the editors and publishers of those periodicals for
their ongoing support of the upland experience.

For Kathleen, The Lady of the House, who has put up with so many canines as well as the person who keeps bringing them home.

And in memory of the dogs:

Meanface Kelly
Pat
Tar
Lee
Kelly
Britt
Nutmeg
Flick
Freya
Huckleberry Finn

and even Feather and Shane . . .

Thanks for leading me astray.

Contents

Preface

ORE THAN TWENTY YEARS AGO, I WAS
vaguely aware of a heck of an outdoor writer
and editor named Chris Madson in the way
writers are aware of each other when they live in the same
state and, in this case, dabble in the same genre. For me,
I think it was a bit of what the writer Anne Lamott called
out so perfectly in her book, *Bird by Bird*: professional
jealousy. Chris was a real writer and editor in the game
of nature and outdoor writing, and I was just toying
with it, supplementing a thin income with the occasional
freelance writing piece in the state's premiere magazine:
Wyoming Wildlife, edited by one Chris Madson. Chris was
in Cheyenne and I was in Lander, and occasionally we
talked on the phone and I sent in submissions—typed
up on paper—and those articles helped me buy shotgun
shells and fuel for my next adventure. I was essentially
being paid as a professional camper, working at a famous
outdoor leadership school, and dreaming of hunting and
fishing pretty much all the time.

After 9/11, I remember thinking I probably needed
to hunker down and work a career where I could make

a little more money and have some upward mobility. It was about this time that Chris advertised for an assistant editor to help him at the magazine, and I jumped at the chance. It meant a move to eastern Wyoming's harsh high prairie from the legendary Wind River Range, but it put me one door down from Chris Madson, a conservationist and writer whose work I admired (and envied). I could learn from him and emulate him. Here was the chance of a lifetime for a would-be nature and outdoors writer to partner with the best in the business. *Wyoming Wildlife*, under Madson's keen editorial eye, was nationally recognized as the top magazine of its kind in the country. Moreover, Chris came to his gifts honestly and genetically, for his father was the legendary nature writer, John Madson, whose stories I had read all my life and whose essay "Pheasants Beyond Autumn" is widely considered one of the best hunting stories of its kind ever written.

Right away, I realized that Chris kept long hours and, immediately, I figured out why. An endless stream of characters would show up at his door day in and day out, plunk themselves down in a chair which Chris often had to clear of manuscripts under consideration for publication, and shoot the breeze about all things outdoors. Chris would somehow edit the magazine between conversations with various office "water cooler" types— some of whom worked in that very building—and others who happened to be traveling down Interstate 25 and stopped off for an impromptu visit with the widely respected editor. This went on day after day and from my next-door perch, I overheard tales of the outdoors *ad nauseum*. Many of those were tales of dogs, and I also quickly realized that few of those visitors could measure up to Chris's knowledge and passion when it came to all things canine. Pretty soon, I was poking my head into his office and relaying a few of my own stories. Then, and still, I ran English setters on upland birds all over the country, while Chris was a Brittany spaniel man.

I also began to realize that Chris, both inside the building and across the country, was seen as something of an oracle in conservation, bird dogs, hunting, and the outdoors. Indeed, it dawned on me that most came to listen to Chris rather than regale.

But at the end of the day, we had work to do, for crying out loud. Steps were necessary.

We enacted a regulation and dubbed it the Solstice Rule. If it were after the close of the bird seasons but before the summer solstice with the days trending longer and longer, we were strictly self-forbidden from talking about hunting, particularly bird hunting. After that late June day, then the gloves were off and we could talk of, and plan for, hunting.

I would not say that we stuck to the rule without hiccup, but I will say that we tried. But more importantly, as much as we both loved to talk and write about hunting upland birds—pheasant, grouse, quail, partridge—behind our bird dogs of choice, we loved to do it more.

Shortly into this friendship, Chris and I plotted a trip up into the great northern prairie country—Montana and the Dakotas—with my pickup camper, my two setters and Chris's Brit, Meg. Two things stick out solidly in my memory of that hunt.

Chris is a man of passion and fire. He loves to hunt, and kill, pheasants most of all. For the first day or two, this enthusiasm was relayed in a manner that began to grate on my nerves. I would be hunting beside Chris, following one or the other of my setters, and he would be perhaps fifty yards away with Meg. Up would go a rooster pheasant in front of me and I would swing the gun, level off and just as I was about to pull the trigger, Chris would scream: SHOOT! I would flinch, miss, and the rooster would fly off cackling. This happened time and again until finally, I turned on the esteemed editor and cried, "For God's sake, would you quit yelling at me!?"

To his credit, he did indeed keep his passion in check— or maybe we started hunting in different directions—and I started to put a few roosters on the ground.

More importantly was the second thing I remember about that hunt. I had a little setter female named Sage, a puppy of perhaps ten weeks, that I was lugging along on the trip to get her some road time, human time, maybe even get her nose full of pheasant scent. She was indeed adorable. I can remember chilly nights in the camper and Chris clucking and cooing to little Sage as if she were the most special thing in the whole world. I think Chris may have even boosted poor Meg onto her dog bed on the floor, then cuddled up to my Sage to sleep in his own bunk. We talked into the dark hours of bird dogs, his and mine. His love of bird dogs was radiant.

In the upland hunting game, there are people who run bird dogs as if they are tools to be kept in a box, taken out, used, cleaned up, and put back. These are the folks who sometimes run packs of bird dogs, kennels full of them. Then there are the Madsons of the world, who cluck and coo and coddle and measure their lives in individual dogs. The dog is a member of a family, and the years metronome by one dog, maybe two, at a time. Or perhaps one veteran and one rookie at a time. This is Chris. *Companions* is aptly named, for the dogs Madson puts on the ground are every bit of that and more. They are partners, kindreds, crucial members of the tribe. Dog is evidence that there is a god. Dog's lack of longevity is evidence that this god is either a cruel one, or one who requires the human to sit up and pay attention to every single moment, for these snippets called canine life are painfully fleeting and gloriously spectacular. That's what *Companions* is about. A life of dogs.

Put another way, the human is lucky, for in a lifetime of hunting, he will bask in the glow of several dogs, a bounty. While for a dog, if fortune smiles upon her, she will only get one human. Hopefully he is a good one. Saint Francis, patron saint of the animals, certainly blessed a dozen dogs with a man named Chris Madson.

The relationship between a hunter and his dog can be an enigma to those outside that oh-so-tight circle. A lot of outdoor writers have attempted to relay that bond in story. Some, like Gene Hill's "Old Tom" and Corey Ford's "The Road to Tinkhamtown" are stories that stand the test of time. Others read like so much puffery and as anyone who has sat around a post-hunt campfire will tell you, there is nothing as boorish as a braggart after a day afield with his dogs. Chris Madson's *Companions* sticks the landing right into the Ford and Hill country. "The Rainbow" is right in the pack—to use a pun—with the best tribute to an old dog ever written. In *Companions* one reads not only of the dogs but of the land, the bird, the partnership, the hunter's duty as a conservationist, the sky, and the wonder of it all. "The Twenty-One" is the best eulogy to a father I have ever read.

I could go on about each story in this book, but I will close with another tale of my friendship with Chris.

In the early 2000s, I had a good tri-color male setter named Ike, the kind of big rangy dog that John Madson called "side-meat and running gears." Ike was a decent enough dog that I had written a story or two about him and those stories had caught the eye of a fan right there in Cheyenne with a fine setter bitch. The reader contacted me and asked if he could breed his girl to Ike. Of course I said yes, with the caveat that I could either take cash or my pick of the litter as Ike's stud fee.

I believe something like thirteen puppies were produced from the romance. One evening, after all the hangers-on had been shooed from the office and Chris and I were putting another issue of the magazine "to bed," I enticed Chris out to look at those pups. Chris's Meg was getting up in years and she needed an apprentice just as I had needed to learn from a mentor of Chris's ilk. I told Chris I would give him Ike's "fee" from the litter. No charge. Just reach into a pile of squirming, soft, licking setter pups and pull one out.

So we went over to see them. We spent an hour or two on the floor being mauled and puppy-chewed by thirteen of the cutest setter pups the creator ever produced. I challenge any person in the world to do that— have a ticket for a free puppy in his pocket—and walk away empty-handed. After this went on for a while and Chris and I were basking in the warmth that is puppy love, Chris rose to his feet, brushed some dog hair off his jeans, smiled kindly at our host and said, "Okay, well, thanks for letting us play with your pups. They are beautiful."

Out we walked.

Chris is, without fail, a Brittany man.

Thomas Reed
Author of Blue Lines *and other titles*
www.mouthfuloffeathers.com
Pony, Montana
Autumn 2022

Introduction:
Old companions

HIS NAME WAS MEANFACE KELLY. DAD
called him that; I'm not sure why—a sense of
the ironic perhaps, since there wasn't a mean
bone in that dog's body. Kelly for short. He was of Irish
lineage, lean and lanky, a rich mahogany in color, but not
to be confused with what Irish setters became in later
years, not the high-strung brainless dogs that prance
through Madison Square Garden for ribbons from the
AKC. Unlike the show dogs of the breed that came after,
he had significant breadth in addition to his length and
height, a quick mind that learned fast and remembered
well, and a setter's calm, affectionate disposition.

I couldn't have been much older than four when he
came to us. One of my earliest memories is the drive
down a long, wooded dirt road in the cool of a spring

evening to bring him home. We grew up and were trained together, and, when the adults let us out, we ran to the fields and creeks with common purpose to drink in the untamed days under a sky that is always blue in my memory and a summer that never ends.

When I was sent to get a carton of milk or a dozen eggs, Kelly came along, his nose at my elbow, at heel across Delmar Street and right up to the door of the grocery store.

"Lie down," I'd say, with all the commanding authority of a ten-year-old boy. And he'd stretch out at one side of the entrance. "Now, stay." And I'd leave him there, without leash or supervision, while I gathered up the items I'd been told to fetch, paid for them, and returned ten minutes later to find that he had not moved. Home we'd go, passing adults on the sidewalk who smiled at the two of us as we went, oblivious of the impression we left behind.

It was the fall semester of my junior year in college, I think, when one of my dorm mates called me to the hall phone.

"It's your dad," he said, as he passed me the receiver.

Meanface Kelly had died, Dad told me—gone in his sleep in the fullness of his years. I mourned him like a brother. Which he was.

After Kelly's passing, after I'd left home, there was Lee, the Brittany, who came into my hands as a three-year-old and Kelly, the sweet-tempered yellow Lab Kathy and I adopted as a favor for a friend. Then, there were the puppies—Britt, the Kansas Brittany; Feather, the sappy golden retriever; Meg and Flick and Freya and, now, Finn, a succession of Brittanies who have led me through so many memorable landscapes, from the windswept blue grouse haunts at treeline in the Rockies, through the foothills and breaks out onto the tawny prairies of the Great Plains, along the brushy fencelines of corn and wheat country, and south into the cholla and catclaw of the vast Sonoran desert.

If those dogs never quite replaced the setter who raised me, they were far more than just pets, more than hunting companions. What we've meant to each other doesn't yield easily to words. So different, the human and the dog, and yet driven by many of the same passions, the same codes of kinship and behavior. Fellow travelers in this life, partners in the great game.

The word "love" has been given many meanings in human affairs, some deep and abiding, others as trivial and ephemeral as a dusting of April snow, the applications so diverse and unrelated that the word is at risk of losing all meaning, except as the context defines it. This context, the bond between canine and human, seems particularly difficult to describe. The affection is undeniable, but there are elements of the relationship that seem to me to be not quite like love—something deeper, bred into the bone, ancestral.

Most of the animals we think of as "domesticated" came into the fold during the Neolithic as humans settled down to the business of farming. The archaeological record suggests that sheep and goats were probably the earliest herd animals to submit to human control, about 11,000 years ago. We've had domestic cattle and pigs for about 10,000 years; horses for about 7,000 years; and chickens for around 4,000 years. Cats? The felines joined us recently, only about 6,000 years ago, which may be part of the reason they have such an independent streak.

By comparison, the origin of our dogs is lost in the mists of the distant past. Canine fossils have been found in several archaeological sites, and, until recently, the scientists who studied those remains struggled to define the difference between the wolves of those far-off times and the ancestors of modern dogs. Since the skulls of modern dogs are generally smaller than wolf skulls, relatively shorter in the snout, and with more crowded teeth, researchers have taken careful measurements of the fossils and, in those measurements, found evidence of ancient dogs.

According to one analyst, a skull found in a Paleolithic campsite in southern Belgium is perceptibly different from wolf skulls of the time. The skull is nearly 32,000 years old. Another dog-like skull, this one from an excavation in the Altai Mountains of Siberia, is carbon-dated at 33,000 years old. As genetic study has become more sophisticated, several researchers have used mitochondrial DNA analysis to estimate how long it has been since the ancestors of dogs and wolves parted ways. The estimates vary widely—one study says the divergence occurred about 15,000 years ago; another estimates a split 32,000 years back, and a third suggests the two may have parted ways as much as 135,000 years ago.

What none of these studies can possibly estimate is the amount of time that may have passed from the first connection between humans and canines and the point at which the canines were recognizably different from wolves. Was there an extended period of time when men and wolves used each other in the hunt without any human control over canine breeding? It's an idea that can probably never be proven, but it's worth noting that Eskimos in search of the often-elusive caribou on the barren grounds of northern Alaska pay close attention to the movement of wolves as the two species hunt for the herds. In all the certainty of our civilized arrogance, we view wolves as rivals or even threats, but that view is not held among the modern hunting cultures who know the wolf best. Robert Stephenson, a biologist who spent years with the Nunamiut Eskimos of northern Alaska, found a much different attitude among those people.

"It is instructive to note that one of the very few remaining societies that has been, and to a considerable degree still is, in direct competition with the wolf for essential food items harbors no animosity toward the animal," he wrote in 1975. "The Nunamiut do not begrudge the wolf its prey."

I see no reason to believe that the attitude of Paleolithic hunters was much different; in fact, I'd bet the respect modern subsistence hunters have for the wolf is a view of long standing, born of a recognition that wolves could be of some help in the human pursuit of game and even that humans and wolves shared a common approach to the challenge of survival.

When "modern" men first wandered north from Africa, the fauna of Europe and Asia was a strange amalgam of animals we know today from the Arctic tundra and the wildlife of the Serengeti, often magnified to a startling degree—lions that weighed in at more than 700 pounds, eight feet long from nose to rump; mammoths more than twice the size of modern elephants; two species of rhinos, each at least as big as the modern white rhino; bears the size of Holstein bulls; hyenas twice the size of the modern African forms; bison almost twice the size of the ones we know today; deer the size of Alaskan moose; ibex and reindeer. The striking murals left to us by the occupants of Chauvet cavern in southern France capture some of the essence of that wilderness, a world nearly unrecognizable to modern humans, 35,000 years ago.

Two species in that menagerie, man and wolf, tackled the problem of survival in much the same way, both hunting big game on the tundra of the Arctic wilderness that was northern Europe and Asia thirty or forty or fifty thousand years ago. Two species with the same approach to the hunt—an extended family led by a couple of alphas, cooperating to out-think and out-maneuver animals that were bigger, stronger, and often faster than the hunters. Both species foraged for berries and other vegetable matter when the seasons allowed, but, most of the year, they lived on fresh meat taken in the chase.

Was there a tradition of cooperation between the two? It's hard to say. Neither the fossil record nor genetic analysis is likely to provide evidence one way or another, but ecologists have found many examples of two species that have settled into a relationship that benefits them both. Oxpeckers gleaning ticks off the backs of rhinos; honeybees, butterflies, moths, and flies pollinating flowers while feeding on their nectar; zebras and wildebeest migrating together, one species with better eyes, the other with the better nose, helping each other detect predators; plovers wandering around the open mouths of crocodiles, fearlessly gleaning food scraps from the teeth of those fearsome predators; ants tending their herds of aphids in exchange for the partially digested sap they secrete. It's not a strain to imagine small groups of Paleolithic hunter-gatherers and packs of wolves learning to coordinate their efforts for mutual benefit, neither one taking responsibility for the other.

It's clear that people first learned the trick of domestication with wolves. I'm inclined to believe that the fossil canines from Belgium and the Altai were, in fact, dogs, not wolves, which suggests that humans were already affecting the breeding of these animals more than

30,000 years ago, and emerging evidence suggests that paleo-hunters came across the Bering land bridge, the gateway to the New World, only 6,000 years later—with their dogs.

In the evolutionary scheme of things, we're a young species, not much more than 200,000 years old, and excavations in Europe indicate that we arrived in that part of the world less than 50,000 years ago. Not long after that, if the age estimates for the remains of the ancient dogs from Belgium and the Altai are to be believed, canines joined us around the campfire. For the next 20,000 years or more, our ancestors and their dogs hunted to support themselves before settling down to a more sedentary agrarian way of life.

That span of time, in itself, is a significant proportion of our entire existence as a species, but I suspect that, long before we domesticated wolves, there was a looser relationship, a cooperation among equals over uncounted thousands of years as we harried the fringes of the great prehistoric herds. That would explain the almost instinctive ability of dogs and humans to read each other, picking up the subtle changes in body language and tone of voice that communicate mood. We may well have been hunting in some sort of association with canines for half our entire history as *Homo sapiens*, and, if that's true, then it might be more accurate to say we evolved with dogs instead of domesticating them.

In the 1970s, a group of archaeologists was excavating a prehistoric village in northern Israel, built by generations of hunter-gatherers who had found ways to support themselves without being constantly on the move. At the door of one of the huts, the researchers found a large slab of limestone and, underneath, the skeleton of an old man, his legs and arms flexed, his head and left hand resting gently on the skeleton of a five-month-old puppy. The two had been buried for 12,000 years.

As I consider the photograph of the remains of those two long-departed souls, I have to think there's an important difference between our relationship with dogs and the ties we have with any other animal. Clearly, we respond to the attention our dogs pay us, their warmth, their feel under our hands. That's an emotion any pet will elicit. But dogs, especially the breeds that share our work and recreation as well as our homes, touch something more. We've been companions across geologic and evolutionary time, through eons in which our struggle for life balanced on the keen edge of a stone spear point, on the success of one more hunt. Our regard for them rises, not only from our hearts, but from our genes, not only from how we feel but from who we are and how we came to be.

Before our sheep and goats and cattle, before the plow, before we began the 10,000-year effort to domesticate ourselves, our dogs led us in another way of life, through the trackless, timeless wilderness before history began. And I wonder, when our eyes meet, whether that moment stirs a latent memory in both dog and man of those long-lost days when we ran at the edge of the great herds and were free. It's a strange trail we've followed to this place and time, a different, tamer world these days than the one that shaped us both.

But, through it all, the partnership has survived. Even now, we share the fire after the evening meal, lulled by the ancient miracle of the flames as they push back the night—two lines welded by common purpose.

Together still.

The essays that follow here have occurred to me over the years, often as I walked behind one or the other of the dogs who've accompanied me through many wild places and times. I put them down on paper in an effort to reach some understanding of the part they've played in my exploration of those places, those times—the landscapes and people that, in retrospect, have been an irreplaceable part of my years on this rare jewel of a planet we all call home.

If you've read this far, I suspect you've had dogs in your life that are as important to you as mine have been to me. I hope that's true, and, if it is, I hope a few of these stories will bring back a memory or two you treasure. I've come to believe that stories are the most enduring measure of the hunt. The memories are what we really pursue.

———————

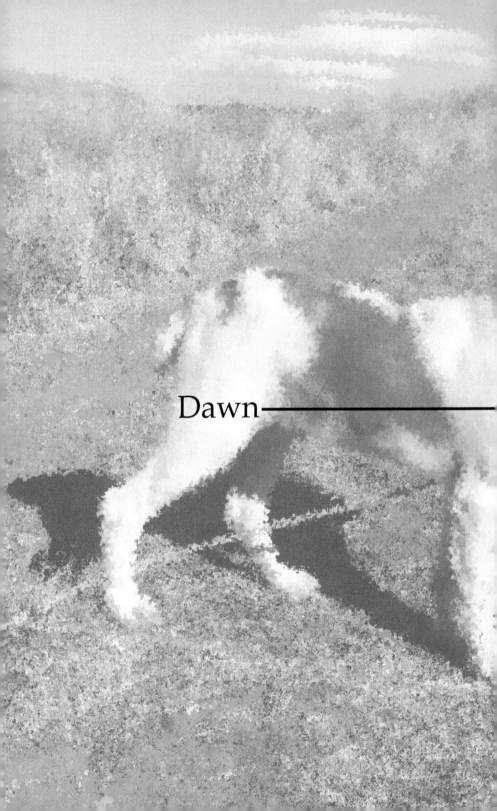

Dawn————————————

Regardless of pedigree and bloodline, regardless of the proven performance of sire and dam, each puppy is an unknown quantity with strengths and weaknesses, few of which are in evidence in his first eight or ten weeks. On the human side of the transaction, choosing a puppy is a leap of faith, an investment in an unforseeable future. On the puppy's side, there is no leap, only the implicit trust in a partnership that will last the rest of his life.

Pointing the way

BILL PUSHED BACK FROM THE TABLE AFTER his second plate of stew and grinned. "Well, I'm about to make your life more complicated. How are you fixed for dogs?"

He knew, of course. Britt, my old male, was snoozing in his dog box, marshaling his energy for the next day. Bill was the reason Britt and I had gotten together. He'd called me when the litter was whelped, and, eight weeks later, I'd made a 500-mile drive to check the pups.

The dam was a beauty, with dual champion credits for three generations on either side of her pedigree. About all that could be said for the sire was that the A.K.C. certified him as pure Brittany. He was tall and rangy for a Britt, and he looked as if a pit bull had sneaked into his mother's kennel at a particularly delicate time.

Still, pretty is as pretty does, as the Kansas farm ladies say. Both sire and dam were superb quail dogs, the pride of a small-town banker who had the run of farms in three counties and spent more time minding the birds than computing compound interest. Bill had followed the careers of all the pups in the first two litters this pair had made, and he swore there wasn't a bad dog in the bunch.

I had my pick of the males in the third litter. There were five, as I recall, all of them as cute as eight-week-old puppies always are, a wriggling mass of warm tongues and floppy ears, already led around by inquiring pink noses. When I patted the ground and mouse-squeaked, one little male kept wobbling over to see me. Bold and curious for such a youngster, he had an interest in humans as well as other dogs, so we went home together.

I would like to believe that my flawless training brought out the best in him, but it would be fairer to say that he was talented enough to overcome the obvious shortcomings of his handler. We started on pheasants, but, before he was through, he hunted bobwhites and cottontops, chukars and Huns, sage grouse, sharptails, blues, and ruffs. When the water wasn't too cold, he retrieved mallards, and one November afternoon, he chased a crippled Canada goose a quarter of a mile over a Wyoming marsh and brought him to hand while my daughter and I watched. After nine years, he was still following that unerring nose wherever the birds led, a little slower but no less enthusiastic.

Bill waited for me to bite.

"Alright, alright, What've you got?"

"I was talking with Jim the other day. He says the

daughter of one of your dog's littermates just had a litter of her own. Nine weeks old next Tuesday."

"Geez, Bill."

"I know, I know—there's never a good time to start another dog. But you know, we're driving right past there tomorrow. Jim wants to look 'em over."

"Well," I granted, "s'pose there's no harm in looking."

We met Jim the next morning, his pickup loaded with a homemade dog box and a little female Brittany, rock hard from a season of bird hunting. Since I was heading the other direction at the end of the day, I followed in my own rig, Britt standing at the back window, whining softly in anticipation.

Ten miles out of town, we pulled into a farmyard. The master of the spread had gone to pick up some lumber, but his wife told Jim to take us out to the kennel anyway. As we walked across the lawn toward the kennel, the dog house emptied out, the female watching us with just a touch of concern while nine puppies fell all over each other on their way to the gate.

"I'm interested in one of these myself," Jim said as we squatted among the pups. "Let's take a couple along with us and see what they think of the cover."

I looked hard at Bill, and he held up his hands in defense as he grinned. "No obligation."

So we scooped up two likely looking young ladies, loaded them in the second kennel in Jim's truck, and drove off into a calm, bright January morning that was just beginning to thaw around the edges—a perfect quail day.

Forty minutes later, we pulled onto a faint two-track that left the gravel just shy of the bridge over a little creek lined with elms and sumac. Like most streams in the Kansas Flint Hills, this one ran over a limestone bottom, spring-fed and crystalline, home to clouds of darters and a thriving population of native spotted bass. It wound through the soft-shouldered hills, disappearing into groves of oak and walnut, then out again past slopes of Indiangrass and bluestem, a sampler of tawny yellow and burgundy in the low winter light. Along the creek bottom, there was just enough milo and corn stubble to sweeten the place for quail.

We uncased guns and headed north along the creek, leaning on the dogs for direction. They meandered through the stubble, crossed the creek, and worked west through a patch of timber, coming at last to the expanse of prairie at the top of the hill. Jim's female pointed hard where the trees gave way to patch of sand plum on a south-facing sloped. I stopped Britt to honor.

Bill swung in on one side, and before anybody could set tactics, the covey exploded. I was too far away to shoot, so I could savor the sight of two exceptional gun hands working a covey. Neither man seemed to hurry— the guns came up in a fluid arc. There was a flurry of shots, and the dogs started their retrieves.

We hunted the singles of that covey with no success; the birds had blasted back through the timber, so it was hard to get a mark on any of them.

As the morning wore on, we worked through one exceptional quail covert after another without finding any more quail. Around one o'clock, we circled back to the truck.

Bill had sandwich fixings and some hot chocolate, which went down well in the cool shade down by the creek. After we had eaten, Jim crawled into the back of the pickup and opened the second kennel.

"Let's take a look at you girls," he suggested.

He scooted off the tailgate with a wiggling Brittany in one hand. Released in the milo stubble next to the creek, she immediately began snuffling over the ground. I went over to the field edge and cut a sumac wand about five feet long.

"Mind if I borrow a wing?" I asked Bill. He smiled and handed me one of the quail. I broke off a wing close to the body, stripped the lace out of one of my boots, tied the wing to one end and knotted the other end to the stick.

"Here, little one." I flipped the wing out on the ground and twitched it a couple of times, luring the pup out of the field. She scrambled over to the feathers and pounced, falling on her chin and somersaulting over the wing.

Bill shook his head. "First time away from mama. You have to give her high marks for confidence," he offered.

I flipped the wing back down on the ground, and the puppy flounced after it again.

"Listen, these are both fine little dogs. If you want one, you pick it. I'll take the other one."

I scooped up the puppy and kneaded one of her ears while she chewed on the base of my thumb with needle teeth.

"Yes, you are a mighty hunter," I told her. "But why don't you give us a chance to look at your sister?"

The second infant was just as bold as the first. I turned to pick up my wing and pole, and, when I looked back, she was already thirty yards down the creek bank, nose to the ground, stub tail vibrating. I squeaked at her and flipped the wing down on the ground. She pattered back with her head up, trying to figure out why she cared about the twitching feathers. As she came up, I let the wing settle. She slowed, took one more step . . . and froze, on forefoot in the air.

It's a tricky thing for an eight-week-old to balance on just three feet, but she managed, wobbling a little as she watched the wing for any sign of motion. I dragged the wing a foot, and she pounced, missing it. Then I laid it out again, and she pointed again. I glared at Bill.

"This is your fault," and I picked up the pup, holding her freckled nose about an inch from mine. "Sweetie, I think you're gonna have to come back to Wyoming with me."

We loaded the puppies back into the truck and took one long swing through the afternoon. We found two more coveys there. Jim's little lady found the first on the edge of a stand of bluestem and held it for two minutes while we scrambled to catch up. Then Britt pinned a second bunch at the head of a brushy swale. He was tired, but the point was high and stylish. The rise surprised me, as it always does, and I rushed the shot, wing-tipping a bird that fell into the thicket, out of sight. Britt disappeared into the brush and emerged a long minute later, a male bobwhite cradled gently in his mouth, bailing out the boss as he had so many times before.

We got back to the vehicles just as the sun dropped over the tall prairie ridge to the west. I cased my gun, boosted the old man into the back of the Trooper, and poured some water for him. He sniffed the bowl, then climbed into the back seat with a grunt and curled up in a tight ball.

"How do you want to do this?" I asked Bill as I walked back to Jim's truck.

"Well, if you want to write a check, Jim can take it back. They'll send you the papers." Bill smiled again. "She *is* a likely looking pup."

I took out my checkbook.

"Do me a favor, Jim?"

"Sure."

"Tell them not to cash this for a few days. I wasn't planning on doing any dog-buying this trip."

"He grinned. "I can do that."

Bill apologized for the ten coveys we hadn't found, and I assured him that good company is better than good shooting—although, I added with a grin, I was hoping we could combine the two someday. We shook hands and promised to rendezvous again in the new year. Then Jim got into the back of his truck and handed me the pup.

"Good luck with this one. She'll do well." And with that, he and Bill headed east.

I made a nest of my hunting coat and down vest in the back of the car, where a puppy's accident would be easiest to clean up. It was going to be a long drive—without a kennel for the youngster, I wasn't going to have the luxury of a motel room or even a snooze in the back of the vehicle. So eleven hours back to the house. I settled in behind the wheel and pointed west.

There was a scrabbling in the back. In the rearview mirror, I saw a freckled nose poke up over the top of the back seat. After a minute's struggle, she tumbled onto the seat with Britt. Charmed to find a parental figure, the little one stuck her nose out to get acquainted. There was a low growl, and the puppy decided this was not her mother. She scrambled up onto the console between the front seats and fell into my lap.

"If you're gonna ride up here," I said, "you better use the other seat," scooting her over. She stretched out as if she had been born there.

As the miles flowed by, I could hear the old man

snoring softly in back, a veteran of many hunts who had given everything he had to give one more time. Next to me, his niece slept the deep, untroubled sleep of the very young. Now and then, she snuffled and her feet twitched as she chased birds she did not recognize through fields she had not yet seen, her mind and heart running true in an ancient course. Youth and experience, promise and perfection.

And it occurred to me that they were not only better than I was at this exercise; they were better than I could ever hope to be. Ultimately, the proof of the hunt lies, not in bag limits or shells burned, but in the quality of the effort we make. It's a matter of focus and dedication, a commitment to a tradition older than mankind itself. Over the millennia, our dogs have led us in that chase, the pursuit of a special kind of perfection.

For those of us who care about hunting, they show the way still.

———

Beginning

THE PURCHASE ITSELF HAD BEEN AN AMBUSH, the kind of trap only a really good friend can set. Bill had heard about the litter and led me in the way of temptation, to which, I will admit, I succumbed with remarkably little resistance. I drove through most of the long night with nine-year-old Britt curled up in the back and the new puppy sleeping peacefully in the seat next to me. She woke up briefly when I stopped for gas in Hays, so I spliced a loop in a length of nylon rope, gave her a quick walk to head off any accidents in the car, and continued down the road, arriving in Cheyenne sometime on the far side of two in the morning.

I managed to get into the house without waking The Lady of the House or our three girls. It's my practice to sleep with a young puppy for a couple of weeks after we get home. Even the boldest youngster is likely to miss the comfort of mother and siblings, especially in the wee hours, and since the resulting distress is bound to wake everyone anyway, I figure a few nights in a sleeping bag on the floor is better than crawling out of bed repeatedly to calm the new arrival. It also seems like a particularly powerful way to strike up a relationship with a new pup.

So, I found the toddler's gate we'd used when the kids were first walking, blocked off the kitchen, and settled down on the linoleum floor with Miss Kansas, who promptly curled up next to my stomach and went to sleep. It had been a long day for both of us.

Four hours later, I heard a soft intake of breath behind me. I cracked an eye. Eight-year-old Tegan, our middle daughter, was staring down at me with a look of rapture I took to be excitement at having her father return from a long trip.

"A puppy!" she squeaked. I felt a warm stirring next to my left cheek—Miss Kansas had found her way to a comfortable spot in the sleeping bag between my shoulder and chin.

"A puppy!" Tegan sprinted off to spread the news to her sisters. My eyes were still glued shut from the drive, and I think I drifted off for another moment before I heard footsteps coming down the stairs.

"A puppy! A puppy!"

I pried my eyes open to bask in the outpouring of excitement and approval from my daughters . . . to see The Lady of the House standing over me in her pajamas.

"A puppy?" she asked, with an arched eyebrow and remarkably less enthusiasm than the children behind her.

It's hard to marshal a coherent response to a question like that after a five-day road trip, after hunting all day in a spot far from home, then driving most of the night to get back. And, as my wits slowly returned, I realized that this was a rhetorical exercise on The Lady's part, that she recognized—of course—not only the age of the new arrival, but its breed, its purpose, and the inevitable effect it was bound to have on family life over the next year.

Lying on the kitchen floor at her feet with the evidence of my misdeed curled up next to my ear, I offered the only defense I could muster: "It was a really good price."

"I'll bet."

"One of Britt's nieces."

"Greeeaaaatt." The word stretched out for what seemed like minutes.

Then, little Miss Kansas performed the very first of many services she would offer her master over her long career. She got up, stretched and yawned, and waddled over to the toddler fence to greet these new people in her life. The girls were entranced, and, as I wandered away to the bathroom, The Lady of the House sat down on the floor and invited Miss Kansas into her lap.

Before the week was out, she was christened: Nutmeg, for the color of her spots and her wacky Brittany demeanor. Meg, for short. Soon thereafter, she visited Tegan's third-grade class and demonstrated the only trick she knew—pointing a pheasant wing attached to a pole with fishing line and flipped onto the floor. Tegan's classmates were impressed by the trick but more taken with the warm, soft bundle of fur that was so very pleased to meet a whole roomful of new friends.

Our walks were short and frequent at first. I made a light check cord out of quarter-inch nylon rope, about twenty feet long, which was plenty to give me a quick handle if little Meg showed too much taste for independence. Which she seldom did. With the check cord trailing behind, she followed her nose from one scintillating scent to another, always watching over her shoulder to make sure I wasn't too far behind. A walk at dawn, then off to my office where she stayed in her kennel until ten. Then, another walk. And an hour's walk at noon. And another short walk at three. And a long walk at six, and another short walk at sunset. You can wear out a pair of boots, keeping a young pointing dog exercised and entertained.

By May, we'd gotten down to three walks a day, an hour each, with maybe ten minutes of training scattered through the proceedings. She only really needed to learn four commands. "Come" was the first. Some say it's the most important, and I suppose that's true, although the second command—"Stop"—seems just about as useful, especially in training a pointing dog. Maneuver her around a signpost, tree trunk, or telephone pole, grab the end of the check cord, and tell her to stop. If she wants to come back instead, stop her with the check cord. She got the hang of it in about three lessons.

The other two commands—"heel" and "fetch"—were a little less important, at least from my point of view, but we worked on them through the summer, until, by August, I could trust her without a check cord.

It would have been a great advantage to work her with live birds, but we lived in town—I had no source for birds. We worked on pheasant wings instead. I'd drop a couple on our way out and bring her up on them as we headed home. As Master Yoda would say, the force was strong with her. She pointed the scent of the wings as staunchly as she had sight-pointed the previous winter.

That left one other matter: introduction to the sound

of guns. I couldn't fire a gun on our daily walks, but I got an idea. I found a piece of scrap hardwood molding from a door I'd replaced and cut it into two pieces, each about twenty inches long. I stapled a short piece of nylon webbing to one end of each piece so I wouldn't lose them and started carrying the resulting arrangement on our walks. When I clapped them together, they made a sharp crack. When she got interested in a scent, I'd crack the boards together, softly at first, then harder. When we worked the wings, I'd use the clapper to form some sort of association between the feathers and the noise. With that preliminary work done, we went to the national forest with a variety of firearms and finished the introduction to the real article.

Dawn on the first of September found us on a section of reclaimed prairie in sight of the high country. Wyoming opens its prairie-grouse season on September 1, and in those early days of the Conservation Reserve Program, the sharp-tailed grouse in the southeastern corner of the state had prospered in the new-found cover. The sun hadn't broken the horizon when I pulled up on the north side of the field, Meg at full attention in the right-hand seat. Not quite a year old, she was no longer the chubby stuffed toy. Lean and hard, long-legged for a Brittany, she hadn't yet grown her feathers and petticoat, but it was clear she meant business.

I uncased the little twenty gauge, slipped into my vest, and lifted her out of the truck before heading south, into the wind. She was overrunning her nose, as young dogs will, but I could see she was paying attention to what the nose told her. I can't imagine what it must be like, the sensory input from that marvelous organ. In the cool of the dawn with a little moisture from a light dew—the lingering scent of every cottontail, jackrabbit, raccoon, ground squirrel, deer mouse, meadow vole, and meadowlark that had passed or slept during the night must have drifted through the cover. Sorting all those, ignoring some and focusing on others, has to be a challenge, even for an experienced dog. Meg was still a rank amateur, aided only by her genes.

And that was enough. As she quartered across the faint breeze, a scent reached out and grabbed her by the nose. She twisted over her left shoulder to stay in touch with it and froze. I examined her body language, skeptical that this was anything more than a mouse, but she seemed lost in the scent, taut as a loaded spring, so I played my part, advancing on her left so she could see me coming. I passed the pink nose and looked down. The amber eyes flamed, locked on something invisible upwind.

There was an explosion of wings. Seven sharptails reached a group decision—they needed to be somewhere else in a hurry. The gun rose; two birds fell, and Meg sprinted out to get the first one.

So many things in the natural world change by slow degrees, almost imperceptible, even to the most careful observer. It's surprising when a change comes instantaneously, like throwing a switch. For Meg, those sharptails were the switch, the moment she left puppyhood behind. Over the next thirteen years, we found many birds in many far-flung places, but in my memory, the rise of those sharptails on that morning has a special place, as clear as if it had happened yesterday.

It was an awakening . . . and I was the fortunate beneficiary.

———

Jaws

SHE WAS THE BIGGEST FEMALE IN A LITTER OF eight seven-week-old Brittanies, a little girl with an almost perfect orange spot on top of her head and the bright, ears-up curiosity of the rest of her breed. Over the years, I've developed a short list of things I look for in a bird dog pup—interest in feathers, interest in people over littermates, an inborn interest in her surroundings. I'd like to believe these traits carry over into ease of training, a connection with the master, and a drive to find pheasants, although I can offer no objective evidence that anything in the behavior of a seven-week-old puppy offers the slightest hint of its performance as an adult.

Certainly, there was nothing that separated any of these eight juvenile delinquents from their littermates.

None of them put up with bullying from their brothers and sisters; all of them were riveted by the sight and smell of a pheasant wing, and separated from the rest, each one came to me when I sat down and squeaked, then toddled off to sniff at unseen trails in the lawn. After nearly two hours of fruitless deliberation, I picked the biggest of the bunch in the completely unfounded hope that she would turn out to be the kind of tall, leggy Britt I prefer for the business of finding ringnecks in lush stands of switchgrass and bluestem.

She curled up in the folds of the dog blanket on the right seat of my pickup without a whine or a single look back, scratched one ear, and promptly dropped off to sleep for most of the twelve-hour ride home. By the time I pulled into the driveway, we already had the beginning of a cordial relationship.

Our household is not new to the raising of puppies. By my count, there have been something like six tamed and trained here. The Lady of the House, known to the dogs as She Who Must Be Obeyed or She Who Clangs (for the time one of the puppies jumped up and smacked his head on the underside of a stainless steel food dish she was holding), was less than enthusiastic about a new pup but recognized that this was part of her husband's obsession and that, as obsessions in helpmates go, this was relatively benign. Three adult daughters were in and out of the house and were overjoyed at the promise of a new dog, especially since they bore none of the responsibility that came along with it.

We were set for the house-breaking, the crate training . . . and the chewing. Or at least, we thought we were. Our eldest daughter rushed right out to the pet store and bought three squeaky toys, which the puppy received with relish. They lasted about five days, which, in our experience, was a fairly rapid attrition rate, but Erin went right back out and bought two more. Those lasted a little more than two days.

Recognizing that this youngster was perhaps more orally motivated than the average puppy, I hustled over to Target for a bag of rawhide chews. These were popular with my old male, Flick, as well as his protégé. Flick guarded the one I gave him, so it lasted about three days. The pup consumed hers in about five minutes.

The little one explored her new home with great care and regularly came down from the bedrooms with dirty socks and used underwear. Some of these items were sacrificed for the pup's entertainment and survived her attention for as much as a week. An athletic knee pad proved to be as pup-proof as anything she appropriated—it took her nearly three weeks to get through the last of the elastic and reach the high-density foam underneath, pieces of which emerged from under the living room furniture for nearly a month afterward.

It was about this time that she discovered the plush pads on the bottom of her dog box. I reached down to let her out one morning to find her lying in a snowdrift of white excelsior, carefully pulled out of a chewed corner of the top pad and teased into a mass that half-filled the crate. I cleaned that out, grumbling under my breath, while she looked on with great attention, pleased to see me down on all fours like an honest canine. She destroyed the second pad during the night.

I was inclined to let her lie on the hard plastic surface for a few weeks until she got her adult teeth, but she supplied herself with a replacement a couple of days later, pulling an Amana wool blanket off the couch and chewing several holes in it. We abandoned the blanket to the dog crate.

Through this first month, the deliberations on a name continued with little success. Feminine French names all seemed too prissy to yell at a misbehaving bird dog: "Fifi, Fifi, come back here you ###**!&*!! dog!" Finally, I settled on "Freya," the Norse god Odin's consort, a female famous in myth for her infidelity and mischievous incantations. The Lady of the House accepted the formal name, but after young Freya destroyed one of her favorite Haflinger wool clogs, she suggested an alternative.

"She's completely crazy, and not really in a good way," The Lady observed. "From now on, she's Ditzy Mayhem for me. Ditzy May for short."

Undeterred by this slight, Ditzy May continued to go through the household like a dull rip blade on a Skil saw. Anything plastic immediately attracted her interest—clam-shell packaging, yogurt containers, empty milk jugs, combs, hairbrushes, garbage sacks, plastic wrap, and anything Styrofoam. One of her early favorites was an empty New Amsterdam vodka bottle from a mini-bar she found along the street during a walk. None of this quelled her appetite for rawhide chews, which she consumed at the rate of roughly three an hour. Nylabones lasted somewhat longer but eventually disappeared, crumb by fragment, down her insatiable maw.

The Lady of the House was worried that she might develop an intestinal blockage, not because The Lady was particularly concerned for the pup but because she anticipated the need for expensive veterinary intervention. As the person who followed after her with plastic bags, I was confident that her GI tract was up to the task, having picked up hundreds of puppy turds spangled with the colors of whatever indigestible item she had shredded and swallowed over the previous twelve hours.

Her appetite was not confined to the sort of things we think of as chewable. Early on, she took it as her sacred mission to chew the rubber ring off the bottom of her stainless steel bowl so that said bowl now slides all over the kitchen floor when she's trying to eat. She chews on the bowl itself as well, along with Flick's steel bowl and the hard plastic bowl that belongs to Jake, the ancient and long-suffering cocker spaniel, who is forced to share the house with her.

Her indoor manners meant that she spent an unusual amount of time in the backyard, where, I thought, there was little trouble she could find, so I was surprised, one sunny afternoon as I headed for the garden, to find her chewing on the clapboards of the house. As part of the ensuing discipline, I put her in the dog pen, an incarceration she had not yet experienced. With her safely confined, at least for the moment, I stepped into the garden next to the pen and proceeded to weed the tomato patch. I became aware of an odd semi-metallic grating noise—she was nibbling on the wire of the chain link fence.

As the first cool days of fall settled over the plains, she conceived an appetite for vegetable matter and, over several weeks, browsed on a number of The Lady's potted plants. Her favorite seemed to be the shamrock. After she had eaten the plant down to its roots, she ate the dirt and then settled down to chew on the ceramic pot.

"It makes my teeth hurt to watch her," The Lady admitted after she rescued the pot.

While the upstairs bathroom was being redone, she watched for a moment of inattention and sneaked in to grab various tools and bits of hardware. Catching her on the stairway one afternoon, I saw that she had her mouth full.

"What have you got there?" I asked suspiciously, at which point, she ran behind the living room couch and spit out a large steel nut for one of the carriage bolts in the project. While I gathered up the nut and stored it out of reach in the garage, she ran back to the bathroom and got the bolt.

Her first lesson on electricity came within a month of her arrival. She was rooting around under an end table in the living room one Sunday morning as we were reading the newspaper. There was a muffled yelp, and she suddenly appeared at my knee, looking for comfort and reassurance. The Lady of the House was immediately suspicious and stalked into the living room to investigate, returning a minute later with the plug and two feet of cord from a string of decorative lights that had been draped over the bookshelves several weeks before. The yelp had been Ditzy's reaction to the electric shock as she bit through the cord.

"Well," The Lady observed grimly, "at least that should break her of biting electrical cords."

Or not. Over the next three months, she severed the smartphone charging cord in my pickup and destroyed a string of holiday lights at Christmas, along with the power cord to The Lady's sewing machine and half a dozen ornaments, including a beautiful Italian angel that had been a gift from one of the grandmothers.

In her ongoing campaign to endear herself to everyone else in the house, she destroyed mittens and gloves, including one of a pair of formal women's evening gloves; ballet slippers; dish towels; wash cloths; shopping bags; pine cones; leashes; shoelaces; PostIt notes; and any piece of wadded up paper she could filch out of the wastepaper baskets or recycling bin. She even mastered the foot pedal that opened the trashcan in the bathroom, showing up from time to time carrying wadded Kleenexes festooned with used dental floss.

On one of her first hunting trips, she managed to get hold of the corner of a Platypus water bladder through the wire of her dog box and puncture it at one corner.

"Where the hell is all this water coming from?" I wondered as I tried to put it in my vest. "Oh . . ."

On the way home, she reached through the bars of her kennel and teased the end of a rooster pheasant's tail feather into reach. Over the next two hours, she shredded all the bird's plumage up to its drumsticks. No harm to the meat, just a half-bushel of Technicolor fibers freed from their quills, floating around the topper.

And when there's nothing else available, she's happy to chew on any finger, toe, or ear lobe in reach—no malice intended, you understand, just Ditzy saying "hello."

In late October, The Lady was assembling a Halloween costume for herself as part of the celebration of the big day at the elementary school where she works. She pulled one of the household's prized possessions out of storage: a cloak she'd made for her youngest daughter's winter excursions at college. On the young student's return, the cloak had been lovingly folded into a Tupperware container of its own and stowed for safekeeping. The dark green velvet reached to the floor, lined with matching green satin and topped with a deep hood that was at once practical and more than a little mysterious, a perfect outer garment for the sorceress in the school library.

After Halloween, the cloak was draped over the back of a chair in my office, waiting to be returned to its storage box. Ditzy found it there one afternoon. I was alone in the house with the dogs when I became aware of an unnatural silence. I turned from the project on my computer to see Ditzy, lying on the floor next to the chair, quietly, contemplatively chewing on the hem of the cloak. She'd managed to destroy about two feet of material along the bottom.

The Lady was still at work, and since the sins of the puppy seemed to settle inevitably on my shoulders, I considered loading my shotguns and field boots in the back of the pickup and setting out in the general direction of Central America. While the plan was still forming, The Lady came through the front door with a sigh.

"That was the day to end all days," she muttered as she set down her things.

"Well," I began, "there's something I ought to tell you." I finished on a hopeful note: "I don't think it should be any problem to repair."

She went down to inspect the damage and returned a minute later without a word, her expression like the face of the Mendenhall Glacier. I considered pointing out that the cloak would have been perfectly safe if it had been returned immediately to its storage box, then thought better of the idea. Ditzy broke the silence with a playful nip at The Lady's coat where it lay on the new living room couch.

"If she touches that couch . . ." The Lady began, looking around for a weapon. I put Ditzy in her box.

She's nearly a year old now. Her permanent teeth are all in, and I think there are some faint signs of incipient maturity, although The Lady doesn't buy it for a second. I had begun to hope that the worst of the chewing might be behind us, until a sunny morning last week.

The rest of the clan had scrambled off to work, leaving me to read the morning paper and do the dishes before retiring to my office. As I was contemplating the state of the nation, I heard a faint scrabble from the kitchen and looked up to see Ditzy prancing toward me with a paring knife in her teeth.

My immediate reaction was to jump up in righteous wrath and whack her for grabbing things off the counter, but the practical problems with that became immediately apparent. She held the handle of the knife firmly in her teeth with the blade sticking out to her right and an expression of playful defiance on her face; she was hoping for a chase around the living room. I went to the fridge and got a piece of hot dog. Offering a reward for this behavior was the coward's way out, I knew, but it at least had the saving grace of heading off serious bloodshed and/or extensive damage to upholstery.

Last weekend, I relieved Ditzy of a nondescript nylon end cap as she trotted through the dining room. The Lady of the House looked up as I tried to identify what was left of the object and shook her head wearily.

"How long do you expect her to live?" she inquired in a weary tone.

"Oh, I don't know," I replied. "Barring an unexpected encounter with a passing truck, another thirteen or fourteen years."

The Lady rolled her eyes and sighed. "Heaven help us," she said as she went back to her magazine.

The Lady spends most of her days at work, so she doesn't see what I see. At almost a year of age, Freya has given up the sudden frantic laps around the living room. After breakfast, she spends an hour or more staring intently through the glass door to the deck, watching the squirrels on the backyard feeder. Occasionally, she retires to her box for a mid-morning nap, and she always waits politely at the front door for her morning walk. Her puppy months are behind her.

As I write this, Jake, the ancient cocker, is snoring upstairs in the living room. Flick, the veteran, is sprawled on the carpet behind my office chair, eyes closed, but alert for any change in the day's activities.

And Freya? Freya is lying next to my bookcase on the other side of the room, a model of canine decorum, musing over the approach of the upcoming bird seasons . . . while she chews thoughtfully on the spine of an eighty-year-old first-edition hardback.

Heaven help us.

———————

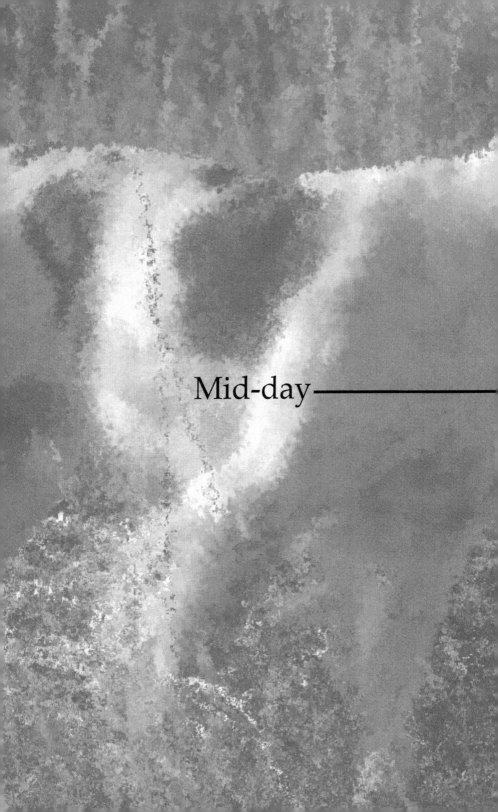

Mid-day————————

It takes time. For some, it's a matter of months; for others, years. It's more than a matter of training; it's a mutual understanding, almost telepathic, each member of the team reading the cover, the weather, the time of day, and each other to form an unspoken consensus on how to proceed. At that point, it's generally a good idea to overrule human judgment and heed the wisdom that has come down to us from uncounted generations of hunters: Trust the dog.

New partners

AFTER I FINISHED MY FORMAL EDUCATION, there was a distressing period when I couldn't find a job in my profession. After three months of full-time campaigning for positions, sending resumes and letters of inquiry to eighty different potential employers, and three interviews where I ran second or worse, I began to realize that any further efforts to land a professional post could be significantly hampered by starvation. To keep the wolf from the door, I applied at a shooting preserve near home and landed a job as a field hand, which entailed a lot of farm work and maintenance in the summer and guiding clients during the hunting season.

The preserve was a cut or two above the typical establishment of its kind. Not far from St. Louis, it attracted professional baseball and football players, state politicians, an occasional Hollywood actor, and even a couple of NASA astronauts. The owner kept a kennel on the premises that campaigned Labs and springer spaniels; at the time, its dog handlers claimed five national retriever championships and three national springer champions. Pheasants were the mainstay of the operation, and, after a long season of watching dogs work, I came to believe that a really good springer may be the best all-around pheasant dog. Even today, I think that may be right.

Now and then, a customer expressed an interest in having his birds pointed. The guys at the kennel were prepared for that eventuality—they had a raw-boned Ryman-style English setter on hand along with two three-year-old Brittanies, William and Lee, brothers out of the same litter, trained on the owner's Georgia quail plantation and sent north. The two Britts had earned their place in the kennel, but they lacked the setter's swagger, the white plume of a tail, so, when the occasion called for a pointer, the Britts generally stayed in the wings while the setter took center stage.

More than a year went by, an entire shooting season and more, before one of my employment inquiries bore fruit. An outfit in scenic Pratt, Kansas, was interested in my services. I gave notice to the manager at the preserve, who didn't seem too dismayed at the prospect of my departure, and I told the rest of the guys that my wife and I would be packing a truck with our meager belongings and heading to the Great Plains just after the new year. They seemed sorry to see me go, and the feeling was mutual—they were all avid hunters themselves, and, together, we'd worked hard to create an almost perfect replica of the discipline we loved. As I walked out to the old Chevy that evening, one of the men who worked in the kennel stopped me.

"Kansas, eh?" he said with a grin. "Good bird country."

"That's what I've heard," I replied. "Looking forward to finding out for myself."

"You could use a good dog."

There was slight emphasis on the word *good*. Two years earlier as I mourned the death of the superb Irish setter of my childhood, I'd bought an Irish setter pup. The owner of the female who had borne him guaranteed him to be one of the new "red setters," bred for the field instead of the bench. He'd turned out to be the worst of both worlds—poor conformation, sparse feathers, a complete lack of bird sense, and an occasional mental short circuit that I found out later was epilepsy.

"I sure could, but I guess that'll have to wait."

He paused a second, considering.

"What do you think of the two Brittanies?" he asked, clearly referring to William and Lee.

"I haven't seen them work. Are they any good?"

"Come over to the kennel the next couple of nights, after the clients are gone. Take 'em out and see what you think."

Since I set the birds for the hunters every morning, I knew where they started and where they settled if the clients missed their shots. The next evening, I stopped at the kennel and took Lee for a walk. On the ride out to the cover, he sat in the right seat, staring straight ahead, all business.

Once upon a time, the preserve had been occupied by a not-very-prosperous farm. The land was seamed with steep ravines, the creek bottoms in dense hardwood timber, the only cropland on the narrow tops of the ridges.

That was where we planted the milo for holding cover. Any bird that escaped the shooters—and there were many—settled in the ravines, a tangle of sumac, scrub elm, and blackberry with occasional openings of broom sedge and little bluestem. It was a jungle no paying customer wanted to investigate. I stopped at the head of one of the ravines, got out, and invited Lee to join me. He trotted into the cover without a look back.

I'd spent the previous two months in the company of flushing dogs—very good flushing dogs, but dogs who were more inclined to pursue than stalk. Lee was a revelation. We'd gone a hundred yards when he turned suddenly into the wind and slowed to a creep, then froze. A springer in the same situation would have shifted into hyper-drive, all his enthusiasm for the scent poured into a sprint and a snap at departing tail feathers. Lee's enthusiasm was just the opposite, a tension so contained and intense that I hesitated to step in front of him. Cursing the fact that I wasn't allowed to shoot this bird, I eased past him and shuffled a boot toe in the grass—a rooster exploded through the low elm branches ahead and disappeared. Lee was staunch to the flush, as he had been taught with quail in Georgia, and I was sure he'd be steady to shot as well.

In the next hour, he pointed another three birds, all with the same passion and discipline. When I got back to the kennel, my friend was finishing the evening chores.

"Well?"

"That was something," I admitted.

"Yeah, they're both fine little dogs. It's a crying shame they don't fit into the rotation here. They'll probably go up for sale pretty soon, but if you wanted to take one along . . ."

Which is how Lee ended up in the right seat of the

Ryder rental truck two weeks later as I drove west, Kath behind me in the Chevy. He was well-mannered but distant, sitting motionless through the long drive, watching the road ahead and never looking my direction.

We rented a little farmhouse a couple of miles east of Pratt, and, by the time we got settled, the upland seasons had closed. Lee was a perfect gentleman—I doubt that he had ever lived in a house before, but he took to the change without a hitch, sleeping in a tight ball at the foot of the bed as the prairie wind found its way through the skimpy walls and windows.

Come spring, I threw tennis balls and sticks for him, hoping that his retrieving was as strong as the rest of his skills. It was. He sat and delivered to hand whatever he'd been sent after. On a whim, I stopped in at the local Alco box store one day and bought a canvas retrieving dummy, just to formalize our backyard exercise. When I got home, I whistled for Lee, told him to sit, and held the dummy in front of him to indicate that this was the item to be fetched. He closed his eyes and turned his head away.

Puzzled, I hid the dummy behind my back and patted him on the head. He opened his eyes, and I threw the dummy. He flinched, and, when I gave him a line and told him to fetch, he refused. There was history here, I realized. Some overzealous wannabe trainer who had never worked with any dogs but Labs had apparently disciplined him with a retrieving dummy. I found out in the succeeding months that the dummy was the only thing he wouldn't retrieve. I had to wonder how his relationship with people might have been poisoned by that one experience.

Summer ripened into fall. On the first of September, Lee and I joined a friend on a shallow stock pond to wait for the evening flight of doves. The shooting was good, and Lee's retrieving was flawless, on land or water. I took him to the marsh for the teal season later that month, covering him with a camo net so that he looked like a Russian peasant woman in a babushka. He stayed motionless on command and fetched the little ducks like a Lab.

At last, the upland seasons opened. I had permission on a dozen sections of land, and we wore them out. The only flaw I could find in Lee's performance was that he was a little too staunch on pheasants. When a rooster decided to run, we worked our way up the trailing scent, Lee pointing every ten feet until I released him. A few of those birds managed to give us the slip, but Lee's gentle approach meant that most of them finally found a hiding place they thought was safe and would hold for our approach.

On quail, he was perfect. The cover in Kansas was new to him, but he clearly recognized the bobwhite as the bird he had first been trained to find. Staunch on the covey rise and the shot, he was unerring on downed birds and generally had a better idea of where the covey had gone than I did.

One Sunday, we ventured farther afield than usual. When the sun touched the horizon, we were fifty miles from home. I made sure he'd had enough water, picked the beggartick out of his feathers, and opened the front door of the Chevy for him. He jumped in, a little stiff after a long day, and took his usual station on the far right side of the bench seat. I climbed behind the wheel and started east into the deepening darkness, a little stiff myself and ready for supper. Lee watched the road a while . . . then eased across the seat, lay down, put his chin on my knee, and went to sleep.

It had been a year since we'd first met—a new person for him in a succession of people, few of which took much interest, some of which may have been less than pleasant. He was far from the land that had given him birth, far from his sire and dam, in country with a different feel and scent, different birds, a strange place in the company of strangers. I'd had no part in choosing his parents, in bringing him up, or showing him the discipline of the chase. I couldn't be proud of him; I was just grateful to have him. And, as he slept, I was glad to know he'd taken me on as a partner.

———

What's worth saving

I'T'S A LANDSCAPE THAT HAS BEEN TAMED. THE wheat stubble stretches out to the horizon over the gentle swells of the high plains, punctuated now and then by a farmstead or, more often, a long-abandoned schoolhouse or barn with empty window frames and clapboards weathered to a dove-soft gray. Down below, the course of the old Missouri with its buffalo bones and keelboat wrecks winds unseen under the blue expanse of Lake Sakakawea. The fierce, feral history of this place has been buried by the plow or drowned.

And yet, it still feels wild. Granted, it is still empty country. If you were to break down on one of these roads, it might be a ten-mile walk to the nearest telephone or a two-hour wait for the first passing pickup. It may be a mile between fences. In late October with the first northers gathering on the horizon, the water skiers and fishermen have winterized their boats and stored them away, leaving the lake to a few private weeks with sun and breeze before freeze-up.

There is something else here as well. The face of the land is easily changed—the wild herds and the people who followed them, the river, the prairie sod were all formidable obstacles, but they were rooted in place, fixed targets. Eventually, they had to yield to the immense mechanical advantage of the technology brought to bear on them. But this place has an essence that has survived domestication. It floats on the wind like cottonwood down, delicate, transient, always just beyond the reach of our machines and ambitions, settling lightly in places where it is not disturbed.

Standing on the edge of the wheat looking down 300 vertical feet or so to one of the arms of Sakakawea, I see what's left of the old times. These are the Missouri Breaks, the hills and ravines that are too steep to plow, too tall to flood. They're covered by the northern prairie's version of savannah. The south-facing slopes support a lush stand of native grasses—I see sideoats grama and little bluestem along with the dried heads of coneflower and gayfeather. The north-facing slopes trend down into thick stands of shrubs standing knee- to chin-high. The snowberries are thick, and the buffaloberries are bending over with loads of scarlet fruit. In the bottoms of the ravines, there are clumps of hawthorn, gray screens of branches tinted with a wash of hot pink—a bumper crop of fruit like tiny crabapples.

Meg surveys the scent along the field edge while I plot a strategy. There will be birds here. The sharptails could be anywhere; the pheasants are likely to be tight in the woody cover close to the wheat. I decide to take a compromise course, fifty yards into the grass, then upwind along the wheat. Meg has finished her fresh-out-of-the-car ricochet and settles down to hunt ahead of me.

We hunt a mile with great expectations. Every hundred yards, there's another promising corner of cover—a clump of buffaloberry; a grassy rock pile; the head of a ravine choked with hawthorn, kochia, and burdock. All good-looking spots; none of them with birds. It's testament to the harshness of this country. In spite of the apparent wealth of food and cover, there's a limit to how many birds this cover will support. Seems a little strange right now, I think—wouldn't if I were here in February.

A cool front is passing. The sky is tangled with clouds, and now and then, a patch of blue and a shaft of afternoon sun. I'm watching one of the patches play over the surface of the lake a couple of miles away when I become aware of a chuckle at the head of the next ravine. A sharptail. The usual quiet rise and rub-it-in call. I run toward the spot, hoping to catch a second bird, but all four have gotten out ahead of me.

It's the first sign that we've come to the right spot. On the next grassy rise, two more grouse flush wild, then another three. I take a fifty-yard shot and miss. The disappearing bird chuckles.

Frustration sets in. Four more birds out of the head of the next ravine. Two more out of the grass beyond. Another long shot. Another miss. The grouse gods don't seem inclined to give up anything easily. And then, a careless single flushes out of the stubble edge, thirty yards out instead of fifty. The sixteen-gauge speaks, and the bird hesitates in the air, then fights to control the fall. Meg makes a seventy-yard retrieve, and the expedition seems more worthwhile.

Half a mile farther on, I angle out into the sparse snowberry on a north-facing slope and find myself in the middle of a stand of bittersweet. Where I grew up in the breaks of the Mississippi, far to the south, bittersweet is a robust vine that climbs its way into small trees—here, it's a single spindly stick struggling for space in the grass. Still, the berry is unmistakable, a yellow-orange fruit like a tiny Japanese lantern.

It's a sign of advancing years, I suppose, But I find memories pursuing me more often than they once did. Dad used to suspend our bobwhite hunts when we came upon a canopy of bittersweet twined into the edge of a patch of timber. I had the honor of shinnying up the trees and doing the cutting. Dad collected the harvest carefully and eased the cut branches into his game pocket. Mom valued the sprigs even more than the quail we brought home. The harvested vines went up around the dining room wall for the holiday season. To this day, bittersweet means Thanksgiving to me.

Dad passed on five years ago, leaving me the sixteen gauge now in my hands and an incomparable legacy of good times in wild places. A quail hunt long past comes back over the years, a warm recollection, a hard loss. A bittersweet moment.

A patch of sun drifts across the grass and moves on, leaving the breaks around me in the flat gray light of late afternoon. Time to head back. We drop down the slope a hundred yards or so and take the contour where the prairie blends into the shrubs. Meg works close and careful in the best kind of collaboration. She's beginning to understand the lay of this new kind of cover and the birds living there—I don't have to make a sound to direct her.

Another pool of sun drifts across the broad prairie hillside in front of us, and the grass turns tawny with strokes of wine-colored bluestem scattered through it. Meg comes up on a low stand of buffaloberry and points hard. I step up to the edge, and five sharptails jump. The straightaway crumples with the first shot, and I swing hard to catch the crossing bird, without success. Meg has already disappeared into the bushes far below me and, after a long minute, emerges again with the bird in her mouth and one wing across her eyes.

It's the last good chance we have on sharptails. We see half a dozen more as we work back over three or four miles of the breaks, but they all flush wild. The clouds have thickened again, and, in the deepening twilight, geese and mallards start lifting out of some secluded bay, heading for feed. Waves of them pass overhead, talking back and forth as they survey the options for supper.

We bump two whitetails out of their beds in the head of a ravine. The forkhorn stops on the edge of the wheat forty yards away to take a second look; the eight-point ducks behind a thick stand of hawthorn before checking the source of the disturbance. Youth and experience.

Then Meg pokes her nose into a buffaloberry patch, scattering the usual collection of juncos and sparrows, and a blur of movement streaks over my shoulder, nearly hitting one of the little birds. After the miss, the form sweeps upward thirty yards or so and suddenly suspends itself over the dog. It has the sleek aerodynamics of a falcon, and, judging from its size, I figure it must be a kestrel.

But a closer look tells me I'm wrong. The bird circles around us, showing its tail, then swings downwind to watch us again. A merlin. This is a new life bird for me. Trim, unafraid, a complete master of the air, the falcon follows us for ten minutes, waiting for the dog to shake more songbirds out of the cover. After two more unsuccessful stoops, she wheels and disappears.

As we skirt the edge of the lake back to the truck, I find myself pondering the wealth of the day. Maybe thirty grouse, several thousand geese and ducks, a couple of bucks, a wild falcon, the endless kaleidoscope of prairie grass and sky—what is this afternoon worth? Generations of hunters before me have defined the value and the currency in which it must be paid. The Teddy Roosevelts and George Bird Grinnells, the Aldo Leopolds and Ding Darlings spent their lives to preserve such places, such days, and passed them on to me.

Up ahead, I see the shelterbelt that runs up the hill to the two-track where the truck is parked. The light is fading slowly toward night, and the quiet of the coming evening is gathering in the shadows. Meg, still hunting, disappears into a thicket of kochia ten feet high, and I hear the oddly sharp slap of a primary on a stalk. A rooster pheasant jumps between two stunted cotton-woods. There's an eight-foot window in the branches; no time to think; snap shot, and the rooster disappears into the jungle of weeds. Even if I hit him, there's no way I can find him. Then the sound of movement in the cover. Meg.

As she steps out of the weeds, the sun drops into the last crack in the clouds at the western horizon, and the land is drenched in the rich butterscotch light of a high plains sunset. The bird glows like molten copper as she drops it in my hand while the last breeze of the day sighs through the branches and comes to rest. For a long breath, it seems as if time has paused. And it occurs to me that Dad is somewhere close by.

Smiling.

———————

Zen in the art
of wingshooting

FLICK LED THE WAY DOWN THE LONG DRAW
with a marked lack of interest—until we came to
the kochia patch at the foot of the old breached
dam. As I watched from the top, he went out the far side
of that jungle with a renewed sense of mission, tail wagging slightly, stopping suddenly when the scent faded,
then zigzagging up the slope as he puzzled out the trail. I
picked up my pace and followed.

We'd gone almost to the top of the hill when he
pointed. I took a deep breath and stepped in front of that
unerring nose. Nothing. I kicked the clump of switchgrass in front of him. Still nothing. He leaned toward the
clump, a sign that he hadn't given up on the scent, but as
the seconds went by, it was clear that whatever had been
there had evacuated. Flick headed downhill to my left,

still intent on a trail, and I started to walk that way when I heard the slap of a primary behind us.

The rooster had looped back and run almost to the crest of the rise, a good forty yards behind me, before he flushed. Like the veteran he was, he hadn't wasted time or energy cackling or gaining altitude; he was no more than five feet off the tops of the grass and maybe twenty yards from disappearing over the hill.

On opening day, I'd have panicked and rushed the shot, but Flick and I were two months and thirty roosters into the season—I'd had enough repetitions to remember again that I had to make haste slowly. Still, the shot was going to be long, and he was going to clear the ridgetop in about four seconds at full speed. Without a conscious thought, I spun around—that awkward turn to the right—and set my feet as the Model 12 came to my shoulder. No calculation, just the rooster sharp against the tawny grass, the strange feeling of time slowing down as I painted through him, the last moment, white-hot, nothing in the universe but the rooster. Flick heard the shot, but when I remember it now, I don't think I did. At the last instant, there was only silence—the sound of the wind in the cover faded away as if someone had hit "Mute." Perfect silence . . . and calm. The silhouette dropped out of sight over the hill.

We both ran up the slope, Flick, because he always runs toward the shot, and I, because it was hard to tell whether the bird would run or even whether he'd been hit. Flick beat me to the top, already busy with his nose since he hadn't gotten a mark. I put my cap down in the general area where I thought the rooster might—or might not—have gone down. Then I followed the dog. We went fifty or sixty yards before Flick decided there was nothing to smell. I turned back, surer with every second that I'd lost this bird. Five yards in front of the cap, my eye caught a flash of bronze in the cover. He was there, his wings spread slightly over the grass in that way that said he was dead before he hit the ground.

I'd like to say I make such shots on a regular basis. After nearly sixty years in pursuit of pheasants and other upland birds, I'd like to believe that. But hard experience keeps getting in the way. A few days after this rooster, a friend and I scattered a covey of bobwhite in some Kansas CRP (Conservation Reserve Program). He marked a single, and we walked over to the spot with his Brittanies until Molly went on hard point, Sophie backing.

Always the gentleman, Ray nodded toward the cover and said, "Take him."

The little cockbird flushed under my feet and flew straight away. I didn't panic, mounted the gun deliberately . . . and missed. Twice.

Over the long drives home in the dark with the dog sleeping on the seat next to me, through the quiet March evenings after the guns are cleaned for the season, during the summer mornings as I walk behind the dogs to keep us all in shape for the fall, I've tried to understand the difference between those two shots and all the others like them over the years.

On the trap and skeet field, a wing shooter can find all sorts of explanations for a miss, followed by endless procedural advice: "Start with a good mount; keep wood on wood (meaning, 'keep your head down, cheek on the stock'); don't look at the end of the barrel; keep the gun moving; give that target four feet of lead . . . ," all important elements in successful wing shooting, elements that have to follow one another in quick succession over the course of maybe four seconds. Trying to check each one consciously off the list as the target escapes at forty miles an hour is a sure way to miss. A beginner trying to execute all of them may not even get to the part where he pulls the trigger before the target is gone.

The reality of the time constraints involved leads veteran target shooters to another observation: "You've got to get your head out of the game—just see the target," as if that's all there is to it. As if it's the easiest thing in the world to tell yourself, "Don't think about that," and then not think about it. But, setting aside how difficult it can be to do, I've come to think this bit of wisdom gets closer to the nubbin of the problem than all the rest. For me, a good shot seems to rise from an unusual state of mind.

Back when I was muddling through college, someone handed me a copy of Eugen Herrigel's *Zen in the Art of Archery*. Herrigel was a German philosophy professor whose interest in Buddhism led him to accept a teaching appointment at Tohoku Imperial University in Sendai, Japan. From 1924 to 1929, he taught during the day and spent his evenings in the study of kyūdō, the traditional style of Japanese archery, with Awa Kenzô, the foremost master of his time, in an effort to understand the mystical ways of Zen as they applied to the bow.

For the first year of his classes, Herrigel stood in front of a large backstop simply learning to draw the bow to Awa's satisfaction; another year was spent on the release of the arrow. Finally, Herrigel gave way to frustration and asked the master when he could start shooting at a target.

"Put the thought of hitting right out of your mind! The archer hits the target without aiming," the master replied. Herrigel responded a little heatedly that, if the master could hit the mark without aiming, he should be able to hit it while blindfolded. At that remark, Awa told Herrigel to come back after dark.

When Herrigel returned, the shelter for the archers was well lit, but the target was in complete blackness forty or fifty yards away. There's no record of the size of the bullseye on the target—modern bullseyes for kyūdō are about 3.5 inches in diameter. Whatever its size, the bullseye and target butt were invisible. Awa nocked an arrow slowly, came to full draw, and after a long moment, let fly. He spent a moment in contemplation, then went through the ceremony of nocking, drawing, and releasing a second time. Lantern in hand, Herrigel walked into the darkness to check the target.

"The first arrow was lodged full in the middle of the black," he wrote, several years later, "while the second arrow had splintered the butt of the first and plowed through the shaft before embedding itself beside it."

Awa said, "Know that it is not 'I' who must be given credit for this shot. 'It' shot and 'it' made the hit."

Much of the rhetoric used to describe and discuss Zen grates on the western mind. I don't know how to define the "it" Awa credited for hitting the mark. In fact, there has been some debate over whether Herrigel's book and Awa's teachings are "real" Zen. I wouldn't know about that.

But somewhere in the Zen search for "detachment," the "everyday mind," or "childlikeness," I see a description of the mindset I have in those rare moments when I make a good shot. The experts at the shooting range are a little off the mark when they say I have to "get my head out of the shot," but they're right in implying that, if there's a little voice making suggestions to me as the butt of the gun comes to my shoulder, I'm less likely to hit what I'm aiming at. In fact, shotgunners, of all people, recognize that "aiming" doesn't work well at all on a moving target.

Practice helps groove the basic motions of a wing shot into reflex, which moves a shooter beyond the need for reciting the list of prescribed actions as he mounts the gun. I wonder if the same can be said of the mental state a shooter is in when he makes a particularly good shot. Can that state of mind be practiced? Awa seemed to think so.

The Zen masters call it "presence mind." The rest of us might call it "concentration" or "focus" or simply "calm." It's a way of seeing that can slow things down in important moments, quiet the voice of doubt, and make the difficult seem possible. Now and then as I follow the dogs through the cover, I'm a little startled to find that things I've discovered there apply to the broader business of life. This may be one. In any case, whatever "it" is, I hope it's there for me next fall.

———————

A few points
on prairie grouse

IT WAS THE LAST HOUR OF THE LAST AFTER-
noon of the last day of the Nebraska upland bird
season, January 31, the leaden sky overhead threatening snow and a thirty-mile-an-hour wind out of the
northwest with an edge like a straight razor. I wouldn't
have been out . . . except that it *was* the last day, and
Flick the Brittany had insisted on one last hunt before
we began serving a seven-month sentence of town
business and home chores that would begin on February 1. So we braved a three-hour drive in the wee hours
of the morning on roads varnished here and there with
black ice and swept with phantasms of snow ghosting
up out of the ditches, coming at last to several familiar
sections of CRP, broken here and there by strips of corn
stubble.

The pheasants had been the way pheasants generally are on the last day. We'd seen seventy or eighty, most of them as tiny specks flying over the next horizon. Flick had pinned two careless roosters over the course of the day, and as I followed him downwind along a low terrace thick with switchgrass, my thoughts were turning to a warm truck and a hamburger when something grabbed Flick by the nose and spun him 180 degrees into the wind.

I cracked the Guerini to make sure there were still two live rounds in the chambers—this was no time to drop the hammer on a spent shell—flexed the fingers of my right hand to get some blood back into them, and walked toward the point, hoping this was a rooster and not some conniving hen hoping to out-maneuver the dog.

Over the years, I've often found that it's unwise to depend too confidently on a prediction of future events. This is a lesson that has general application to the business of life but is especially relevant in the art of wing-shooting, a lesson I ought to have mastered about fifty years ago, in this context, at least. Still, when I step up to a pointing dog's ear, I bring certain expectations, which are often unwarranted and generally lead to failure.

This was nearly one of those moments. As I took the first step beyond Flick, certain that a rooster was about to explode out of the grass, there was a giant rush of wings as ten or fifteen sharptails erupted in a shower of snow. The gun started to my shoulder of its own accord while I fought the temptation to shoot into the middle of the flock, almost impossible to resist since I'd been expecting a single target. Then, the birds slowed and the wind faded out of consciousness and time itself paused as I focused on one shape at the edge of the flock, saw him, really saw him, managed a smooth swing through him . . . and saw his wings fold. Flick was already on his way as the gun came down and I watched him pick up the bird as the rest faded toward the gray horizon.

To this day, I don't know quite what to make of those birds. The fields I was hunting that day had seen a lot of dogs and men over the preceding three months. Even the hen pheasants had learned to flush at 300 yards and fly over the next rise before landing. Most days, as discouraging as it is to admit, sharptails and prairie chickens are even wilder than pheasants. By rights, the sentry in that flock should have seen me as I came over the hill a quarter of a mile away. He should have taken off at that first sight, leading his brethren into the next county, chuckling as they went, to add a dose of insult to the injury of their early departure. That's what prairie grouse do.

Except when they don't.

I could make a fairly convincing argument that, most days, a serious prairie grouse hunter would be better off without a dog. In my experience, both sharptails and prairie chickens spend most of the fall in sizeable flocks with many suspicious eyes always watching for approaching danger. It's not unusual to see a sharptail perched in a shrub or low tree, a sentinel for the birds on the ground. Finding prairie grouse isn't nearly as tricky as finding pheasants or quail; the challenge is getting close enough for a shot. A dog ranging out ahead often does little but increase the distance at which the birds flush, particularly when the dog in question is a member of a wide-ranging pointing breed who can bump a hair-trigger flock before he even catches their scent.

And, again in my experience, prairie grouse are much more sensitive to wounds than the typical pheasant. A crippled sharptail is much less inclined to run when he hits the ground, and the ground he hits generally has thinner cover than most pheasant coverts. A shooter who gets a good mark on a downed bird is likely to find it without canine assistance.

But I'd rather hunt birds without boots than without a dog, and it was clear that, on that one January afternoon, at least, I'd have walked past the sharptails without Flick. I suspect the weather was part of the reason we got within gun range. The birds were hunkered down in a thicket of switchgrass in the lee of a low terrace next to the corn stubble where they had fed that morning, and we came up on them almost silently, just one man, one dog, no talking, no whistles, an absolute minimum of noise and that tiny bit covered by the sound of the wind.

There at the end of the season, Flick and I had worn off most of the rough edges. He kept track of me without need of command, and, when I decided to change direction, I could catch his eye and cue him with a hand signal. The stealth approach was a good way to catch a pheasant unawares, even better for sharptails.

Common wisdom is that prairie grouse hold best early in the fall, when the birds of the year are young and the big flocks haven't yet gathered. For that reason, most prairie states open their seasons long before they allow hunting for other upland species. Depending on the state, prairie grouse may be legal game for almost two months before pheasant and quail seasons open, when broods of young birds are less flighty. A good time to wear the tallow off hunter and dog and take advantage while advantage is to be had.

I recall a sunny September morning in southwestern Nebraska—Britt the Brittany and I were strolling through half a rolling section of Conservation Reserve grass with grouse on our minds. Britt was young and inclined to bump birds, but on this morning, he took one large swing out into the grass . . . and froze. I thought he'd probably cornered a badger but walked up to check. He was adamant, and, as I stepped in front of his nose, a pair of camo-colored birds erupted, no more than fifteen yards away. The obligatory pause while I tried to decide whethether they were hen pheasants . . . or something else. Definitely something else, I thought, as the gun came up. Early sharptails—a special time with a special bird.

Come November, the coveys of sharptails and chick-ens are large and suspicious. If prairie grouse behaved like bobwhite quail, it might be possible to spook one of these flocks to break it up into smaller, less daunting pieces. Alas, prairie grouse are endurance fliers, unlike the white-meat quail and pheasants. When a flock takes wing, it may not come down for miles. When one of my Brittanies points a sharptail or chicken this time of year, it's almost never part of a sizeable flock.

Which is not to say it will be a lone bird. Three times last season, I walked in on solid points to see a single prairie chicken flush just out of range, and let down my guard, only to have one or two more birds flush ten yards closer. I suspect these small bunches were parts of larger flocks that had been flushed a mile or two away and spread out over the landscape. The first time I missed the opportunity to cash in on one of these "hang-ers," I reminded myself that these grouse are social birds, not often caught on their own. With that admonition in mind, I have no explanation whatsoever for my failure to mount the gun on the next two occasions.

If there's any good news in prairie grouse behavior for the owner and operator of a pointing dog, it is that chickens and sharptails would much rather fly than run.

I can't recall ever following one of the those point-relocate-point-relocate sequences and finding a prairie grouse at the end of it. Even bobwhite quail are more inclined to slip away from a point than the typical prairie grouse. And since these birds seem able to fly forever, there's not much chance a green pup will ever run under a tiring bird and catch it. A couple of sprints after a dis-appearing flock will convince an errant youngster that chasing is a fruitless exercise.

Compared to the postage stamp of real estate the average rooster pheasant calls home, the range of a sharptail or prairie chicken is gigantic. When a really serious blizzard roars out of the north, a sharptail may move forty or fifty miles to find shelter in a prairie bottomland while the pheasant quietly freezes to death within a few hundred yards of where he hatched. For that reason, I find it more than a little strange that, where I see prairie grouse on a given patch of cover one week, I may well see them again the next. These core areas shift from year to year, as they do with most upland birds, but it's worth remembering an encounter early in the season because there's a decent chance it won't be the last in that spot. Whether they hold to a point depends on the delicacy of the dog's work, the mood of the birds, and the luck of the moment.

I've seldom hunted prairie grouse as a main course. My encounters with them have generally been an unex-pected aperitif at the beginning of a long walk after pheasants on the Great Plains or as dessert at the end of one of those days. I wish I'd been around before the plow to see the flocks in their uncounted thousands, sweeping low across the prairie on a December evening. As it is, the birds that remain are a reminder of a wilderness that was—which is worth quite a bit, in and of itself. And, when they rise in front of the dog, the stories of those distant times rise with them and reach out to touch the present—the birds, the dog, and the hunter suspended in time. Some things are slow to change. Some of the best things . . .

———————

Fool's hens

TWO CHANCES ON TWO BIRDS: THE YIN AND yang of dusky grouse hunting.

Flick the Brittany and I started almost at treeline, working our way down a broad mountain ridge sparsely covered with scrub lodgepole pine on top where the soil was little more than gravel, dense spruce and fir on either side. We'd walked half a mile when Flick slowed down and went up on his toes. I followed his intense gaze and saw a male dusky grouse on the ground in the dense limbs at the base of one of the lodgepole clumps. He was walking slowly away from the dog, put-putting in mild alarm. Flick pointed, moved a step or two as the bird moved, pointed again, relocated again, the grouse drifting around the edge of the clump, the dog responding ever so carefully.

I lengthened my stride to get between them, my thumb on the tang safety and the little twenty gauge at the ready. The bird decided, at last, that he wasn't going to be able to walk away from this dual threat and flushed.

I may not be quite as fast with the gun as I once was, but I'd guess he hadn't gone ten yards when the barrels caught up with him. Just as I pulled the trigger, he took a sharp right turn around the lodgepole thicket. A shower of needles drifted downwind as Flick ran over to check on the result, disappearing around the trees, then re-appearing with a disappointed look.

Anyone who's tangled with ruffed grouse in the Lake States knows that evasive maneuver—the suggestion of a straight line of flight, then the instant bank around the nearest screen of vegetation, as if the bird has a perfect plot of your line of sight. He vanishes at the instant you slap the trigger; a shower of leaves and twigs settles to the ground . . . and you go on, the dog looking back at you, a little disgusted with your performance, then returning to the business of finding more scent.

Which is what we did. Twenty minutes later, we were in a stand of ancient spruce with an understory of the little green-stemmed herb they call grouse whortleberry, for good reason, since, in season, the birds dote on the leaves, stems, and berries. Flick was out of sight up the slope as I picked my way along a game trail and came, suddenly, unexpectedly, nose to beak with two young grouse who were strolling in my direction. They stopped. I stopped. Maybe ten feet between us. I took the shotgun off my shoulder, held it at port arms, and stepped for-ward, ready for the explosion.

They turned around, walked up the trail ten feet, and stopped. I advanced, trying to look menacing, ordering them to fly. They walked ahead of me, bobbing their heads and put-putting to each other while I did my best to convince them to fly while keeping my feet under me for what I knew would have to be a quick shot.

We went fifty yards up the trail this way until we came to a huge deadfall. The bole of a giant spruce had finally cracked and toppled, bringing down a tangle of branches and smaller trees, a brush pile that was impenetrable for anything bigger than a grouse. The two bent down and disappeared into the pile. I whistled for Flick, and, just as he appeared, I heard the sound of wings on the other side of the deadfall where the slope steepened and fell a thousand feet into a heavily wooded canyon. I had no idea where they'd gone.

A high-risk strategy, I thought, this business of walking ahead of a predator until you're out of sight, THEN flying. It's why they call them fool's hens, I reflected, but, on further consideration, it occurred to me that they might not have been the fools in our encounter.

Most serious ruffed grouse hunters I know back East wait for the leaves to fall before they load up the dog and head for the aspens, rightly concluding that it's easier to hit a flying bird when you can see it. Most of the leaves never fall in dusky grouse habitat. There are nearly always screens of spruce and pine available to hide a dusky's flight when he decides to fly and a remarkable amount of shrubbery, low branches, and deadfall to protect him when he prefers to walk.

I once thought that a dog simplified this problem a little. A dusky grouse may never have met a human, but he's had plenty of experience with coyotes, bobcats, martens, long-tailed weasels and other four-footed hunters. For that reason, a dusky grouse is more likely to fly when pursued by a dog than by a human.

Trouble is, the bird will nearly always run a bit before he flies, which often means he sets sail out of sight, disappearing into the timber with remarkable speed, often down a steep slope, leaving the hunter with no mark for a follow-up. This walk-before-I-run tactic is frustrating enough for a flushing dog—it can almost ruin a young pointer.

Not all dusky grouse are so touchy, of course. Since they've learned that coyotes don't climb trees, they often flush just ahead of a dog and fly up to the nearest available branch, maybe fifteen feet off the ground, maybe fifty, where they perch calmly to study their pursuers. I've thrown rocks and branches at them to get them to fly, even shotgunned the branches on which they sat, hoping to get a chance at a flying bird with the second shot. Generally, they just bob their heads and move closer to the trunk. When they do fly, I'm usually left with a renewed appreciation for just how hard a forty-yard snap shot at a bird flickering through the canopy of a spruce forest can be.

Dusky grouse are moving targets in more ways than one. As a very general rule, adult males tend to stay high on the mountain year-round. Many hens head downhill after courtship in the spring, sometimes moving clear out into the sagebrush grasslands below the timber to nest and hatch their broods. I suspect this migration has to do with the abundance of insects they find at lower elevations—like most other young birds, dusky grouse chicks require a high-protein diet in the first six or eight weeks of life, which means bugs.

Meg the Brittany and I met one of those sagebrush families on a sunny afternoon in early July as we scrambled down a precipitous ravine that led down the flank of a canyon to a stretch of river no sane fly fisherman would ever try to reach. A healthy stand of aspen shaded the spring-fed trickle that had carved the ravine while the cool north-facing slope was covered with an almost impenetrable stand of spruce and fir, the deadfall under the trees so thick a pine squirrel could spend a lifetime without ever touching the ground.

We picked our way along a faint game trail that wound its way down through the sagebrush and fescue on the sunny south-facing slope. Meg had outgrown her interest in voles and ground squirrels, so, when she pointed a particularly dense clump of sage, I slowed down and watched the cover for any sign of movement.

After ten seconds of this tableau, a female dusky grouse stretched her neck to peek cautiously over the top of the shrubbery, trying to figure out why this potential predator hadn't pounced. Still unsure of just what she was facing, she walked slowly away, bobbing her head and clucking softly. As I watched, five smaller shapes emerged from the cover.

The youngsters weren't even half the size of their mother, still partly covered with down, but, as I watched, one of them took flight, fluttering into the aspen below, followed by its four siblings. The hen continued to walk away from the point, probably in an effort to distract the dog from the brood. After she was certain she had our attention, she flew across the ravine and disappeared into the spruce somewhere up the hill from her family.

She'd picked a good place to raise a brood. These days, much of the sagebrush steppe at the edge of the West's conifer forests is grazed down to the subsoil. The sagebrush itself struggles to survive, and the carpet of grass and flowering plants that once grew in the shade underneath is gone, taking with it the assembly of insects that allow a young dusky grouse to grow from less than an ounce at hatching to more than two pounds in just three months. This brood was lucky, I thought as I contemplated the wildflowers growing up through the sage in this isolated seam in the canyon wall. Plenty of protein among those plants, and enough cover to shelter the brood while it looked for bugs. In a couple of months, there was a chance Meg and I might meet this bunch higher up the mountainside.

As the nights cool off and the youngsters learn to fly, the hen leads them uphill into the timber where they spend the fall and winter, feeding on berries and a variety of green stuff at ground level until the snow flies, when they move into the trees to eat the tips of conifer needles. Safe from predators, except the occasional passing goshawk, their feet may not touch the ground between November and April.

The timing and intensity of this uphill movement varies with individual hens—when they hatched their broods, what food they find at lower elevations, and, apparently, their general mood. I know it's happening, and I try to allow for it, but there's a lot of real estate on a western mountainside, and, in most years, not all that many grouse.

The practical way of determining how high on the mountain the broods have gotten on any given day is to drive the back roads and scout. I've done that, but it always feels a little like cheating, since it can quickly devolve into road hunting. I prefer to pick a ridge where I've seen birds before and walk it with the dog. On many days, this approach only confirms a basic ecological truth about the western mountains—year in, year out, they're not all that productive. It takes thousands of acres, spread from the sagebrush to timberline, to support a population of dusky grouse. It's possible to spend a lot of time and boot leather looking for them without much finding.

I'd like to believe I've developed a sense of the vegetation the birds prefer—the corners that have a little more moisture and support the whortleberry and other plants I find in the crops of the occasional bird I put in the bag—but, when I visualize the places I've actually met dusky grouse, they run the gamut from heavy, mature spruce timber to sparse second-growth limber pine and lodgepole, stands of ancient Doug fir, the edges of meadows, forest openings whose gravel and rock support no more than a few wisps of grass and broad-leafed plants. Dusky grouse are where you find them. About the only rule of thumb for locating them that occasionally helps me is to look where I saw them last year.

If I'm lucky enough to have a tracking snow for the elk season in mid-October, I may see a few grouse tracks, but, as the snow deepens, the birds abandon the ground entirely and spend the winter in the canopy above, browsing on conifer needles. They're picky about their diet, choosing trees whose needles contain relatively few indigestible chemicals. A preferred tree may take on a slightly "hedged" look by the end of the winter as grouse nibble the tips of its needles. High up in a dense stand of conifers that provide shelter as well as food, a dusky grouse may actually gain weight between November and April, a rarity among the wild residents that winter in the mountains.

For ground-bound predators like Meg and me, snow makes dusky grouse unhuntable. Once the high country turns white, we head to the prairie where the walking is easier and the birds, a little less challenging.

As I consider this litany of frustration, I find myself wondering why I bother with dusky grouse. I guess the most obvious reason is that, where I hunt them, the season opens earlier than it does for any other game bird besides mourning doves. By the time September arrives, the dogs and I are both anxious to get on with any activity that may yield a bird.

But, in spite of the frustrations involved, there's much to be said in favor of the pursuit of dusky grouse. They may not be as gaudy as a ring-necked pheasant, but they have their own, more subtle, beauty, a medley of slate blue and gray that echoes the shade under the big trees that shelter them through much of the year. They're a white-meat bird nearly the size of a young pheasant, with the delicate flavor of quail, a prize on any table.

Mostly, though, I hunt them because of where they live—the black timber and lonesome ridges of the Rocky Mountain West. It's a way of getting to know the high country unlike any other. A way of seeing. Feeling. Such places are a pleasure and an education in their own right.

The birds are a bonus.

Bet your boots

THE SUN WAS ON THE WESTERN HORIZON when we got back to the truck. Freya the Brittany was walking just behind me, her head down, limping slightly on her right front leg. She looked the way I felt. We'd been on the road three hours before sunrise, and the dawn had found us in a quarter-section of CRP that, just five days before, at the end of a blizzard, had been stuffed with birds.

That was then. In the intervening five days, the sun had come out, and the always-fickle gods of the high plains had seen fit to offer a preview of spring—bright sunshine, hardly a breath of wind, and afternoon temperatures in the low fifties. Everybody in town was ecstatic. The dog and I were less enthused.

The warm weather meant that the late-season

roosters could be anywhere, from the shady depths of a juniper windbreak to a quarter-section of corn stalks beaten flat by cattle. We started in a patch of kochia that had held sixty pheasants the previous week—this day, there was a single hen. After that, we hunted three of our best coverts and failed to stir a single bird.

As the shadows lengthened in the afternoon, Freya pointed in a waterway overgrown with canary grass. As I came up behind, she started to creep along the ditch, flash-pointing, then checking the scent and easing cautiously forward. A runner. The bird jumped about twenty yards ahead and flew straight into the afternoon sun. By the time I saw color, he was on the shady side of fifty yards, in high gear. I flung a shot at him out of frustration and watched as he sailed over the ridge to the south, untouched and triumphant. That was the sum total of the day's action.

I gave Freya half a can of dog food and a bowl of water, then sat on the tailgate and changed out of my field boots, which, by that point in the day, weighed about thirty pounds apiece.

There was no doubt—my morale had taken a hit. I've chased pheasants for something close to sixty years now, and I'd like to think that, over all that time, even a Scowegian like me would start to have a feel for the right places to look for birds, considering the weather, the season of the year, the time of day, the cover, the hunting pressure, and everything else that affects a pheasant's choice of haunts. Nothing I'd tried on this day worked. It's tough to admit to being out-maneuvered, out-run, and generally out-thought by a bird with a brain the size of a kidney bean, but there it was.

As I sat, watching the sun go down and resting my feet, I reflected on the nature of pheasant hunting. It is, in many ways, a game of chance. The skilled player improves his odds with a knowledge of probability and his opponents, but on any given deal, his options are determined by the way the cards fall. If the hand is bad, he can choose to fold, and if his luck runs cold, he can always surrender his chair at the table and take up another pastime—bowling or checkers or the football playoffs. But if he decides to play, he risks his stake.

And what, I thought, was I risking today? I looked down at the boots. The rough-out leather was polished smooth and turning black; the stitching on the side seams was beginning to fail; there were seeds and bits of dried leaves wedged under the frayed laces, and the lugs on the soles were worn almost smooth. How many miles of switchgrass, bluestem, kochia, goldenrod, ragweed, and brome had it taken to reduce those boots to that condition? I had no idea. More than I cared to think about.

Guess that's what I'm willing to bet, I thought. Make the best call I can, then back it up with the willingness to walk to the back of another section, to work cross-grain across the corn stubble and shove my way through the switchgrass and kochia thickets. To persist through the empty hours and never lose focus.

Hunters talk a lot about ways to succeed in this endeavor: strategies for early season and late, when the birds are out to feed, when they're loafing in the cover, how to put the sneak on a cattail patch, how to set up the drive on a crop field, where the birds head during a storm and what they do after, how to recognize the best cover at different times in different places. And the rest of what passes for wisdom among pheasant hunters. It's all worth bearing in mind, although, as the years have gone by, I find I know less and less for sure about pheasants and their ways.

But this much I know for certain: A good dog will help. And a good pair of boots. In the end, the game is a gamble—our time and effort against the native sagacity and toughness of the birds we seek. We bet the endless miles against the chance that a rooster will make a mistake.

Win some. Lose some.

———————

Immigrants

IF TATMAN MOUNTAIN WERE IN CENTRAL Nebraska, I thought as I plodded toward the top, it would be world-famous—which, I supposed, was a sort of back-handed lesson concerning the effect of a poor choice in companions, for mountains as well as humans.

To the west, the first ridges of the South Absaroka Range rose out of the sage, only twenty miles from where I stood, the slopes black with elk timber, the highest peaks hidden behind towering walls. Off to the east, the rampart of Wyoming's Big Horn Mountains crowded the horizon, the snow-capped spine fifty miles away but sharp as a serrated blade in the clear October air. In such company, Tatman Mountain is really just a foothill but formidable nonetheless, especially when one is climbing up through the badlands on the south side with a shotgun over the shoulder and an extra ten pounds of water in the back of the vest.

Britt and I had come looking for chukars and gray partridge. I'd heard reliable reports that the populations had exploded the previous year, reports I should have followed up just as soon as they'd come to me. As the autumn slipped inexorably toward winter, I kept thinking we'd investigate, but, every week, there was another emergency at the office or a complication on the home front. Before I knew it, the world was celebrating the beginning of a new year, and I was mourning the end of the bird season.

But hope springs eternal. The following October, I found an unoccupied weekend, and Britt and I headed northwest to see what had become of the previous year's abundance.

Generations of Americans have nursed an abiding urge to bring game birds from the far reaches of Europe, Asia, and Africa to the New World. The success of the transplant of the ring-necked pheasant from the Far East to western Oregon fueled their ambitions while the difficulties with earlier pheasant introductions in New York and other eastern states were generally ignored. The generations of struggle that finally established self-sustaining pheasant populations in places like the Dakotas and Iowa were likewise dismissed, as were the failures of pheasant transplants in many other parts of the United States.

In the years following World War I, federal and state wildlife officials took up the challenge of importing new game birds with steadily increasing enthusiasm. The experts were convinced they knew enough about exotics to find places in the New World that matched their homes in the Old.

Turned out, they didn't know nearly as much as they thought. Efforts to establish dozens of other species of pheasants, quail, partridge, and even guinea fowl nearly all failed, giving emphasis to the basic ecological observation that transplanting exotic birds and mammals is not only a bad idea but generally doesn't work. Two species—the gray partridge (also known as the Hungarian partridge or Hun) and the chukar—proved to be the exceptions that proved the rule, and even these two species struggled in many places. Between 1931 and 1970, chukars were released in forty-one states, but, by 1968, they had established themselves in only ten western states and Hawaii. The gray partridge was released in more than thirty states but currently occupies parts of just fourteen.

From an ecological point of view, the good news is that neither species displaced a native counterpart. The gray partridge is most common across the northern edge of the Wheat Belt where it manages to survive on landscapes that have been converted from grassland to grain. Once upon a time, these prairies supported sharptailed grouse, but the natives mostly retreated with the grass, and, these days, even the Hun struggles to maintain a foothold in much of the country it had apparently settled fifty years ago.

The chukar found a completely unoccupied niche, if it can be called that when no other living thing had been able to survive in it. I've never laid eyes on the chukar partridge's homeland in central Asia. I hear it's steep, broken, waterless country, a tough place for anything to survive, which must be why chukars have made themselves so comfortable in the steep, broken, waterless country of the arid West.

Tatman Mountain fits that description—a clay hogback eroded out of the sediment from the surrounding mountain ranges, its flanks a steep tangle of knife-edge ridges and deep ravines, its summit a narrow strip of anemic sage and rabbitbrush sparsely watered by the occasional spring seep. A lonesome place, home to a scattering of giant mule deer bucks, a band of wild horses . . . and, after a couple of mild winters and an unusually wet summer, a bumper crop of chukars and, now and then, even a surprising number of Huns.

I was banking on the possibility that the previous year's largesse had carried over. When Britt and I got to the top, we worked west along the rim. Chukars like steep places, and it had been my admittedly limited experience that they preferred to walk or run uphill and fly down and across. The rim, I thought, would give them an instant escape route, which they would keep nearby to use, with a minimum energy outlay, in the event of an unexpected emergency.

As we crested a low rise, Britt stopped. I eased up behind him and looked out over the grass tops to see several chukars on alert at the cliff's edge sixty yards ahead. The cover between us averaged about four inches high with plenty of bare gravel between plants. I doubted that Britt could pick up much scent in the crosswind, but he was locked on the sight of the sentries.

It was a standoff. None of the participants on either side wanted to disturb the delicate equilibrium. I looked down at the twenty gauge over-and-under in my hands, improved cylinder choke and modified. A sprint toward the covey was unlikely to reduce the range of the shot by more than ten yards before the birds flushed, which wasn't nearly enough. The only other option was what I think of as the "hands-in-my-pockets, whistling-a-tune" approach in which I pretend not to see the birds while angling toward them in a casual, lollygagging sort of way, looking the other way, and commenting, to no one in particular, about the weather. On big game and flocks of geese, this actually works. Sometimes. Occasionally. I'd never tried it on upland birds, but . . .

Under my breath, I told Britt to "hold," while I stepped up on the ridgetop and sidled in the general direction of the chukars. Out of the corner of my eye, I saw the sentries stretch their necks while a dozen other heads popped up out of the sparse cover. I redoubled my imitation of nonchalance and got three steps closer before the whole bunch dived over the edge of the cliff, out of sight before I could have raised the gun and out of range in any event.

Britt decided he was free to approach the scene of the evacuation, snuffling as he came to reacquaint himself with the unusual scent. We both peered over the edge, wondering where the birds might have gone and contemplated about twenty square miles of possible destinations, each one as likely as the other. Out-maneuvered. Again.

So we went on, ambling along the rim as the day unwound toward evening. There were some old chukar droppings scattered here and there in the dwarf sage, evidence that my choice of cover hadn't been entirely mistaken, and some ancient sage grouse droppings as well. I assumed the bombers had moved down the mountain to a stock tank or the edge of the irrigated hay-fields along the Greybull River ten miles to the north—some place that offered a little water. The hours passed, and nothing moved on the landscape except the dog, the hunter, and the feral west wind.

We worked our way around the giant table that was the top of the mountain and were headed back when Britt's ears perked up slightly and his nose twitched. As I watched, he trotted off to our left with a new sense of purpose, and I followed in the forlorn hope that this was something more than old jackrabbit scent. Two hundred yards on, he suddenly disappeared.

It was a small pocket just where the tableland crumbled off into thin air, an almost perfectly hemispherical defile that looked as if it had been excavated by design rather than formed by nature. The sagebrush on the flanks was three times the height of anything else we'd seen that day, and a lush stand of basin wild rye covered the bottom, apparently rooted in some source of moisture. In better times, I thought, there's a spring here—I wondered whether the dip had been formed by some kind of subsidence brought on by the action of groundwater. Whatever its origin, the spot seemed like a garden of Eden hidden by design on this high desert promontory.

Britt was not inclined to contemplate the geology or ecological significance of the place. He was focused on a scent, which apparently led around the rim of the bowl at the edge of the taller sage. When he reached the other side, he pointed, no more than forty yards from where I stood.

I was skeptical. This didn't feel like chukar cover, and, even assuming that a bunch had decided to roost here for the night, it was hard to believe they would hold this well. Still . . .

I took off my gloves and eased around to Britt's point. He was insistent—no turn of the head as I came up behind him, no relaxation of a muscle or movement of the tail. Whatever he had, it was close by. A step in front of that quivering nose. Another step . . . and the explosion. A dozen birds or more, practically underfoot, all on the wing at once, all headed for the horizon at top speed.

I'd been expecting chukars, and, as the gun started up, there was an instant of confusion. Not chukars. Not dickey birds. Huns!

In retrospect, I blame that microsecond of confusion and ornithological inquiry for the miss. It's possible that I didn't quite get the comb of the stock to my cheek and/or that I didn't completely focus on the first bird. Having missed with the first barrel, I rushed the second shot when there was no need and watched the group drop over the edge of the table, unscathed.

It was still a long way back to the truck, and, with no sign of any more game birds, there was plenty of time to reflect on the day's lessons. The tutorial in wingshooting was one I'd audited many times before, although it was clear that I hadn't fully grasped the essential elements. Some of the other findings were more ecological—and less painful to contemplate:

The books say that, at least in America, the gray partridge is a farmland bird, tied to the sparse cover at the edge of wheatfields on the northern plains. The Huns Britt had pointed clearly harbored a different view of proper gray partridge habitat.

Ten miles or more from the nearest hayfield and much farther from any significant fields of small grain, these birds had found a way to survive and even thrive out in the western grasslands, like miniature sage grouse, but without the sage grouse's ability to digest sagebrush leaves. They must have been eating the seeds of native grasses like the wild rye where we'd found them. It seemed like a precarious way to make a living, and I wondered if their presence was an accident brought on by a succession of soft winters.

A second ecological insight concerned the nature of game bird populations, especially in the cold deserts of the West. It's an unusually harsh landscape. Natives, like the sage grouse, have evolved a relatively conservative lifestyle. Adults live relatively long lives and are less prolific than many other game birds, compensating for their low reproductive rate with a longer reproductive life. The combination helps the population make it through the hard years when cold or drought can addle eggs and kill downy young. Even so, the population graph of sage grouse is a roller coaster of highs and lows, a response to the punishing conditions in which they live.

Imports, like the chukar and Hun, are committed to a more profligate approach, which means the highs in their populations are, if anything, even higher than they are in gentler environments and the lows, far lower. A female chukar may lay a dozen eggs—in a good year, nearly all of those hatch and the young make it to November; in a bad year, almost none of them do. The gray partridge is even more prolific, laying fifteen eggs or more in the season's first nest and renesting repeatedly if the first clutch is lost.

Both species live fast and die young—before their first birthdays, on average. They overcome their astonishing death rate with a reproductive potential that is nothing short of explosive. Boom and bust is a normal state of affairs among small game animals in the sage, whether the creatures involved are native desert cottontails and grouse or imports like the chukar and Hun. One banner year is no guarantee of another, especially in the West.

Which led me to a decidedly non-ecological observation: When the word of a good year whispers through the ranks, it's best to clear the calendar, whistle up the dog, and go in search of it. Such gifts are rare and never last long; it's best not to ignore them. Neither the gods nor our dogs are inclined to forgive such foolishness.

Discovering the desert

"THERE!"

I held up an index finger as the sharp whistle evaporated in the saguaro.

"Nope," Harry came back. "Phainopepla."

And the bird repeated itself, just to rub in my mistake.

The subdued winter conversation continued out in the brush; a goldfinch, a towhee, a flicker in the distance and half a dozen other voices I didn't recognize. Then, at the edge of hearing, far up on the ridge, three notes, accent on the middle syllable.

"Chi-CAH-go!"

As we listened, there was an answer from the mountainside behind us. Harry grinned.

"Which bunch do you want?"

Neither side was a bargain. When the Gambel's population hits a high, the desert overflows with quail, coveys in every ravine, birds picking gravel in the two-tracks and hanging out in the ditches.

This was not one of those years. The coveys that had survived the summer and fall were in strongholds, the coverts up away from the road where a tiny spring waters the filaree and a buckthorn thicket offers an easy escape. Here, in the broken land south of the Mogollon Rim, those secret spots were mostly far up the side of a mountain. Hunting Gambel's quail late in the season in this country is a lot like hunting chukars farther north—if you want to get in amongst them, you'll probably have to climb.

The cover on the west side looked more open from the road, so I saddled up with a vest full of water, uncased the little twenty gauge and opened the pickup door for Flick the Brittany.

This place was utterly new to us both—saguaro and barrel cactus, teddy-bear cholla and staghorn. The morning felt like June in the northern prairie we call home, even though the January sun hadn't yet appeared over the eastern horizon, and I weighed the idea of chaps for me and boots for the dog. After a moment, I decided the chaps would be too hot and the boots, too much hassle.

We crossed the dry wash and made our way through the sparse vegetation on the other side, heading for a deer trace that led up the face of the ridge.

Thirty yards up the trail, I made my first acquaintance with catclaw. Flick and I are both used to sharp stuff standing between us and birds—the Kansas prairies have their sand plum thickets; Iowa, its raspberry tangles; and the High Plains, their carpets of sandbur and prickly pear.

We both knew enough to steer clear of the cholla, but the delicate sprays of catclaw arching over the trail seemed innocuous enough … until I tried to push past one. When the thorns dug through my Levi's, I stepped back, directly into a clump of white-thorn. As brief as that introduction was, I immediately conceived a deep respect for both shrubs and went out of my way to leave them undisturbed.

Which wasn't that hard in most spots. The vegetation on the south slope was thinly scattered over bare ground and bedrock. As we zigzagged up the hill, the first sun touched the top of the ridge, the rich orange warmth pushing the cool blue dawn down into the canyons on each side. The little cock bird up above quit declaring his sovereignty and went to breakfast, but by this time, I had a good mark on him. Flick quartered uphill, and I followed, one step at a time, up, always up.

When we got to the top of the first ridge, I saw why the birds liked it. A fold on the other side was choked with scrub oak, some of it ten feet high, all of it impenetrable, even for the dog. A fringe of native grass had set seed along the ridge top, and after the rains of the last month, there was a blush of green in the shade, sprouts of filaree and other forbs responding to the moisture.

Quail food.

Flick had already made a couple of sweeps along the edge of the shrubs. In his professional opinion, the birds had moved up the ridge. I had the feeling we needed to go the other way, but over the years, I've learned the hard way that it's not wise to ignore the findings of Flick's nose. How he could pick up scent on that baked clay and scree was beyond my understanding, but he was convinced and I wasn't going to argue.

A flash point. I hurried to catch up, but he was

moving again, a sure sign that the quail were running. It's hard to sprint with twenty pounds of water and shotgun shells hanging from one's shoulders, but I did my best, which meant that I was in full stride when the covey flushed at about forty yards.

I don't do my best shooting when I have to slam on the brakes, set my feet and shoulder the gun. At least, that's my alibi. I saluted the covey with two shots that had no effect except to emphasize that my intentions were serious. Panting, I reloaded just in time to catch the two birds that nearly always refuse to flush with the main bunch.

One of those birds stayed behind.

I've spent some time reading about Gambel's quail. I've looked at a lot of very nice photos of them and watched them stroll around the feeders at the Arizona-Sonora Desert Museum and wander through suburban backyards in Phoenix, and I have to say that those facsimiles of Gambel's quail bear no more resemblance to the genuine article than a Pomeranian lap dog does to a gray wolf.

The covey had scooted ahead of us like miniature roadrunners, and when it was clear that Flick was following them, they'd exploded through the cactus at something close to the speed of sound, tiny gray wraiths against a gray-green background, hard enough to see, let alone shoot. By sheer accident, they'd flown across an open spot just before they landed, which gave me a mark. I whistled up Flick and we followed.

It's been said that Gambel's quail never hold to a point, which seems to me to be true about ninety percent of the time. If the covey's together and the cover is sparse—and in Gambel's country, the cover is sparse more often than not—the birds are likely to run and flush wild. But, if the covey is broken up and a few birds find cover that makes them comfortable, they may hold surprisingly well.

That's what happened when we followed this bunch. Flick pointed a clump of grass, and I made it almost to his stub tail before the pair jumped twenty yards ahead. Another bird stayed behind.

The two of us worked steadily higher on the mountainside, chasing the occasional "Chi-CAH-go" above us. At one point, a mile from the road and almost 2,000 feet higher, we heard three coveys at once, scattered across the face of the mountain at the head of a drainage. I picked the lowest of the three, climbed up even with the call and eased across the south-facing slope on the contour to come in just above the birds.

Flick led the way over a sharp side ridge, and when I followed, I found myself at the edge of a grove of paloverde, so thick at waist height I could barely force my way through it. The lowest couple of feet were almost open, so Flick trotted out of sight, nose down, intense, and two seconds later, I heard the covey leave, invisible in the tangle. No shot, no mark on where the covey landed—completely out-thought and out-maneuvered by birds with brains the size of sweet peas.

And so the day went, up and down the ridges, the view shrinking to a tangle of shrubs, then opening to a twenty-mile vista in the low winter light, the saguaro with arms raised, surprised to see a human on the mountainsides they usually shared only with their quail. The load in my vest steadily dwindled as I kept Flick hydrated and burned shells, mostly to no effect.

The highlight came on a steep slope 200 yards above the main wash. The two of us circled around a crack in the rock, a narrow defile that dropped almost vertically below us, choked with paloverde and buck-thorn where an ephemeral spring sometimes watered them. As we turned the corner, Flick pointed, just as a single quail flushed. I snapped a shot at him as he disappeared around a shoulder of rock, and Flick took off in that direction. I reloaded and took a second step, at which point another bird jumped to my left. No thought, just the little cock plunging down over the tops of the paloverde and the pop of the shot, distant in the moment of concentration. The bird folded and continued his fall, disappearing at last into a thicket at the bottom of the crack, seventy yards below.

That's a lost bird, I thought. Dog didn't get a mark on him, and even if I had, I'm not sure I could get down there, let alone force my way into the brush. And where's Flick anyway? I waited, and after a long couple of minutes, I heard his bell, almost out of earshot, from the bottom of the ravine down below. As I watched, he scrambled up out of the brush onto the scree, then up the near-vertical lava face on the right, struggling for a foothold. With the bird in his mouth. He topped out ten yards from me, dropped the quail and disappeared to the right, looking for the other bird.

They were the last birds of the day. An hour before sunset, we rendezvoused with Harry and his dog, and the four of us eased ourselves into the truck, dogs curled up tight in the back seat, hunters resting their feet up front. Back in Harry's trailer, we got dinner working, then sat down on the floor to pick tiny cactus spines out of the canines. When I'd finished with Flick, I stood up and dropped my jeans to extract half a dozen that had made their way through the denim into my own thighs. Then a plate of Harry's exceptional baked halibut fillets with cheese sauce and to bed.

As I pulled my toes up in the bottom of the sleeping bag to keep the cramps out of my calves, I thought about the process of getting acquainted with a new piece of country. Over the years, I've struck up that new relationship in many ways: a morning drive on the back roads, a hike up a new trail, a birding expedition at dawn, a float trip, all of them fine introductions in their own ways, different approaches to the same end.

If they have a flaw, it is that they hold me at arm's length from the land. I feel like a tourist or a voyeur, peeking through a window at things somehow beyond my reach. Hunting is a different way of understanding the land: more demanding, more intimate. The silence of a wild place is infused with the pulse of process, the ancient flow of energy between predator and prey. The hunter is not a visitor; he is a participant. And so the quail teach me something about living I wouldn't otherwise grasp. There are many ways to learn the desert, but this must be one of the very best.

———————

The Twenty-One

THE HOUSE I GREW UP IN HAD MORE THAN ITS share of amenities—fishing poles and a skiff with a well-kept set of oars; a rangy, tick-ridden setter with a special affection for children; a resident covey of quail in a raspberry thicket out back; and several hundred acres of oak timber owned by a well-heeled local entrepreneur who was gone more often than he was around and abandoned his woods to the local kids.

We were feral by day, slipping into the kitchen at odd hours to feed ourselves, then disappearing for hours on end, only to show up at dusk, sweaty and mosquito-bitten, to help set the supper table. After everybody was fed and scrubbed, we settled down to stories.

Dad was a writer and a lover of words. Every wall in the house was lined with books. Most evenings, he'd take one of my little sisters in his lap, and the rest of us would gather on the floor to follow the exploits of Brer Rabbit and Mowgli, Tom and Huck, the Two Little Savages, and, later, the Devil and Daniel Webster, the castaways on Mysterious Island, and the man-eaters of Kumaon.

We weren't poor by any stretch, but I can remember dining on macaroni and tomatoes or bread and white gravy for several nights at the end of particularly lean months. There clearly wasn't room in the budget for acquisition of gilt-edged firearms, as much as the old man might have coveted them.

There's no doubt that he had a taste for classic shooting irons. Sometime after he left the Army Air Corps and before he took on the fiscal challenge of housing and raising a family, he'd traded for a Winchester Model 75 Sporter, a tack-driving bolt action .22 that executed scores of fox squirrels in his hands, nearly all of them shot in the eye. He was the proud owner of a Colt Woodsman, surely one of the finest .22 automatic pistols ever conceived, and a pre-64 Winchester Model 70 in .243 that would clip the flea off a groundhog's ear at 300 yards.

The Twenty-One materialized in the back of his closet with absolutely no fanfare when I was about eight, the endpoint of a transaction that was wrapped in secrecy until the day the old man died. It was officially a Winchester Model 21, one of the most venerated of side-by-side double-barrels from the classical era of American gun-making. This example of the breed was an ascetic little twenty gauge—no engraving, no inlay, just a gold trigger and an ivory bead, twenty-lines-to-the-inch checkering and that classic line, like a greyhound caught in mid-stride.

It weighed in at six-and-a-half pounds, which explained the first time I ever handled it. When the old man decided it was time for me to learn to point a shotgun, he reached for the lightest gun in the house. The fact that it was choked Skeet One in both barrels was also an advantage for a beginner—at twenty yards, the pattern had already spread to better than thirty inches.

I got pretty handy with that little gun before he weaned me off it. One April afternoon, we went out with the hand thrower and a couple of boxes of targets to burn some powder. When we were set up, he pulled a Model 12 out of a gun case and handed it to me.

"Where's the Twenty-One?" I asked with some dismay.

"Home. You know, Tiger, that gun is a little short in the stock. I've always suspected it was made for a woman. You've grown over the winter. Last time you shot it, I thought you were gonna catch your nose on the top lever."

"But you shoot it."

"Sure do," he said with a grin. "That's 'cause it's mine."

Over the next few years, the Twenty-One taught each of my little sisters how to hit a flying target, but when the lesson had been learned, the Twenty-One reverted entirely to its master.

According to the serial number, it had been built sometime in the mid-Thirties, but in the field, the old man handled it like a newborn. When we had no choice but to bust some brush, I'd watch him shield the stock with his forearm, and when the day promised to lead us through a few raspberry tangles or bois d'arc hedges, he took another gun. Same thing if the day threatened rain. Or snow. The Twenty-One was a fair-weather firearm, and every time it was touched by a human hand, whether for show around the house or duty in the field, it was lovingly stripped down and gone over with cleaning rod, cloth, and the best gun oil money could buy.

Choked as it was, the Twenty-One was a specialty gun. It wasn't much use on pheasants and even less effective on ducks. The old man took it out for the opening of most dove seasons, figuring the birds would be working fairly close and wouldn't take much killing. Now and then, we'd chase woodcock in the river bottoms when the flight was in. But, mostly, it was a quail gun, in fact, the perfect quail gun.

The old man was an unusual marksman. He grew up shooting rabbits and squirrels with a .22 so that, by the time he was out of high school, he had an instinctive skill with rifles. I used to watch him shoot rabbits on the run with a .22 pump, "feeling for 'em" with the first couple of shots, then rolling them as they hit high gear.

For some people, this early experience with rifles might have been a handicap when it came to shotguns, but the old man made the transition flawlessly. Most Saturdays, I spent the morning on the porch of the gun club, nursing a cold cream soda, while the old man shot trap and skeet. He didn't have the time or cash to make the big shoots, but once he'd paid for a round of targets, I think he wanted his money's worth—it was the rare clay bird that hit the ground in one piece.

In his hands, the Twenty-One was lethal on a covey rise. When I was smaller, I'd walk along with him just to see the country and act as chief porter, carrying birds and straining to keep up. When we walked into a covey, it was like a grenade going off, feathered shards flying every direction at hypersonic speed, scaring me out of several months' growth. The old man stood in the middle of that chaos with the Twenty-One, in slow motion, the gun coming easily to the shoulder, popping twice, and back down again as he broke the action and fed in two more shells, without looking. Then, we'd pick up birds.

Eventually, I got to carry a gun on these expeditions, first, a single-shot twenty, and then a Model 12 Featherweight in twelve gauge. Young reflexes and eyes being what they are, I got pretty good with that pump after I'd learned to quell the flinch when the covey rose. The old man allowed as how I could get three shots out of that pump about as fast as any human that ever lived, occasionally even hitting what I was shooting at.

One November in my seventeenth year, the two of us were hunting the limestone-ribbed hill country that stands between the lower Illinois River and the Mississippi. We'd just crossed a dilapidated barbed wire fence that separated a strip of corn stubble from a hillside of broom sedge, russet and orange in the afternoon light, and were making our way toward the sumac and timber at the top of the ridge, fifty yards away. We were the first hunters the covey had seen that fall, I'm sure, and we walked right into the middle of it before the birds flushed. I'd been expecting birds in that place, with the muzzle forward and my finger on the safety. The gun came up as the birds came up—I could see the pure white on the cock bird as my cheek settled on the comb— and just as quickly as it had started, it was over.

I walked to my mark to pick up the bird, then looked at the old man.

"Did you shoot?" I hadn't heard a report, not even from my gun.

He smiled as he broke the Twenty-One, reloaded, and walked up the slope to the first bird, then across a low limestone outcrop to the second. Two in the time it had taken me to kill one.

"It's that gun, y'know," I said, half kidding, half nettled at being out-shot . . . again. He nodded thoughtfully.

"Can't argue with that."

Not long after, I headed off to college and work and a family of my own. As the years went by, we'd get back as often as we could, grandkids in tow. The holiday visits were particularly memorable. Sometime between Christmas and New Year's, weather permitting, the old man would arrange at least one afternoon of shooting. The younger set had a chance to demonstrate their prowess with the .22, closely supervised by a phalanx of parents, and the older kids got their first look at clay targets. The Twenty-One was there to assist anyone whose arms were a little too short for the bigger guns.

After the shooting was done and supper had been served, the aroma of warm mince pies mingled with the unmistakable perfume of Hoppe's Number 9 as the old man tended to firearms, the Twenty-One last and most carefully. As I admired the beautiful lines and unblemished simplicity all over again, he'd look at me over the top of his glasses wistfully.

"It's a great little gun, alright, but I've always thought it was made for a woman."

We hunted together now and then—ducks, pheasants, and quail in Kansas; doves on occasion; and once, an expedition for mule deer in the Wyoming high country—but those moments were few and far between. The old man was much occupied with his work, and I was pretty well taken up with mine.

One Saturday in the spring of 1994, the phone rang. It was the old man. We chatted about the weather, which was already hot, and the fishing, which was warming up as well. He asked after the grandkids, already in high school.

"Funny thing happened on the skeet field today," he said finally. "Stood up on Station 1, raised the gun, and couldn't keep it up. Something wrong with my left shoulder."

"The dreaded torn rotator," I said.

"Yeah. That's what I figure, too. I'll go see what the doctor can do for me in the morning."

He went, and the doctor said he needed some pictures, so they made an appointment with the MRI folks in St. Louis. A couple of days later, the results were back.

Bone cancer.

I visited as often as I could over the next several months. There wasn't much that could be done except control the pain. The doctors were giving him some high-octane medication for that, but the medicine clouded his days, and I suspect he was more inclined to hurt than live what he had left in a fog. Still, in all our talk, he never mentioned a word about himself, about the disease or what the doctors were saying. He wanted to know about the family, about work, about the predictions for the next bird season and the fall flight of mallards. He was more interested in living than dying, right down to the end. It was an object lesson in holding onto grace under pressure—just what I would have expected from him.

A couple of days after the funeral, my mother gathered us all together.

"We need to talk," she said. "Dad had some things he wanted taken care of." We covered all the sad business of wills and what went to whom. We're a close family, and there was no difficulty in any of it—we were all much more concerned with what we'd lost than what anybody stood to gain.

"And as for the guns," Mom finished, "I want to hold onto the Woodsman. You can draw straws for the rest. Except for the Twenty-One. He wanted that to go to Kate, as eldest daughter."

I nodded. It was a right thing.

"How will I get it back to California?" Kate wondered. "We flew here, and I don't want to try to take it back on the plane." She thought a moment and looked up at me. "You're closer to us than anybody else. Why don't you drive home with it, and we'll hand it off the next time we meet?"

"I can do that."

So the Twenty-One rode to Wyoming with my family and me. When we got back to the house, unloaded, and got everyone fed, I took it down to the basement, stripped it, and gave it a thorough going-over to make sure all the handling of the last week hadn't left any stray marks. The bores were mirror bright after a couple of passes with the lambswool cleaning rod, and nothing spoiled the satin perfection of the blue steel.

Except . . . As I started to put the forearm back on, I saw a slight blemish on the left barrel, just where the steel met the wood. I swiped at the mark with an oiled rag, certain that it was just lint. The mark stayed. I peered down through my reading glasses. The trace of a fingerprint, just the edge of it, where the left hand falls when the gun is mounted. The acid from the print had made its way through the bluing down to the bright steel, which is why it was visible. No rust, just the delicate white stencil of someone's identity, left only a month or two before.

It could only have been the old man's. No one else was ever allowed to clean the Twenty-One; very few were allowed to handle it. Sometime, just before his last visit to the hospital, he'd taken the gun out of its hiding place, to admire it, maybe, and evoke the memories that clung to it, all the bright November afternoons with the autumn haze blurring the far ridges, the scent of cured leaves on the breeze, and the grass, still damp from the morning's frost, breathing the aroma of the good earth below, the cool, rich loam settling down for a winter's rest after the fevered pace of a long growing season.

In ordinary times, he would never, ever, have left that print, and as I contemplated it, I could see into those last months—the ebbing away of strength and attention, the loss that came with every new day. The pain. As he'd handled the little gun that last time, he'd done everything he could to live up to the standard he'd set for himself over a lifetime, and the tracery of the print showed that, in the end, his body had failed his will, even in this, one of the smallest disciplines he lived by.

The gun turned gray and blurred in front of me as I considered the only record of that intimate moment, etched on the barrel. No—no salt tears on the blue steel. That would never do. I reached for a pad of 0000 steel wool above the reloading bench. With a little gun oil and some careful work with the steel wool, I could erase this tiny evidence of my father's weakness.

And then it occurred to me that there was nothing of weakness in that mark. I wiped it down thoroughly to make sure it didn't find its way farther into the steel, slipped the forearm into its place, and put the Twenty-One away.

The following summer, Kate and I met at the headwaters of the Clark's Fork of the Yellowstone with our families to spread the old man's ashes on the water. We figured the river knew where he should rest better than we did. When we got back to camp, I took out the

Twenty-One and showed Kath the print. Soon after, the gun went on to California.

There are moments in human affairs when craft rises to the level of art. In the 1930s, the craftsmen who built the Twenty-One blurred the distinction between the two, combining flawless function and durability with grace and undeniable beauty. It's a monument to the idea that, if something is worth doing, it's worth doing well.

The old man shared that view. Over his lifetime, he gathered more than the usual quota of friends. He was an excellent field companion, a gifted storyteller, and rock-solid in a pinch. He was loved and admired for all those reasons and for something more. He reminded us that, done well, living itself is an art worthy of our most concentrated efforts. As far as I know, he never wavered in that conviction, and even in his last days, he gave it his best. It seems right that the Twenty-One will always carry his mark—an owner who appreciated the little side-by-side for what it was and, even more, for where it led.

Judy's cranberry chocolate chip bread

I PROBABLY SHOULD HAVE KNOWN. DECADES OF hard experience have taught me that the success of a hunting trip is inversely proportional to the distance I have to travel before I uncase the shotgun. When I committed to the rendezvous, I was fully aware that it entailed a 500-mile drive. Jim was looking at just under 800 miles. But this, I thought, would be an exception to the rule—four days of pheasant and quail shooting in the wilds of central Kansas on private land that had been scouted and graded by our host and dear friend, Ray, and his two deadly Brittanies, Molly and Sofie. Generous to a fault, Ray had saved the best for his guests. How could this fail?

Jim and I arrived just hours before one of the nastiest storms of the winter descended on the central Plains.

When we rolled out for the first morning's hunt, the thermometer stood at eleven below, and a forty-mile-an-hour wind was driving light snow against the north side of the house. According to the National Weather Service, the combination put the wind chill at about thirty-five below. The experts claim that, in these conditions, frostbite begins to affect exposed skin in about ten minutes. I wouldn't argue.

Undaunted, we donned insulated bib overalls, grabbed extra stocking caps and mittens, and loaded into Ray's ancient Suburban for the trip to the first covert, confident that our endurance would be rewarded, that the birds would hold tight as ticks, that we would be back at the house with limits inside an hour.

The birds had other ideas. Most of the pheasants had taken cover in places the dogs couldn't even find, and the roosters that remained insisted on flushing a football field away. The quail had retreated to that secret tunnel they have leading from Hoisington, Kansas, to some unknown location in southern Texas. We walked and froze, and at the end of two days, Ray had managed to kill four roosters; I had two, and Jim had yet to fire a shot.

The third morning broke clear and almost tropical—according to the thermometer on Ray's back porch, the temperature had risen to zero, and the wind was no more than ten miles an hour. We took our time over breakfast, waiting for Wayne, a mutual friend, to show up. He arrived promptly at eight, and we prepared to launch the two-vehicle convoy to a couple of CRP patches Ray had been saving. As he threw the Suburban in gear, there was a knock on the front window, frosted with the breath of hunters and dogs. Ray cranked it down.

"Here," Wayne said, shoving a foil-wrapped package into Ray's hands. "You boys need some of this." And with no more comment, he jumped back in his truck.

Ray smiled as he handed the package to Jim.

"Every time we hunt, Wayne's wife, Judy, sends along a loaf of her cranberry chocolate chip bread. You haven't lived 'til you've tried some of this."

Jim peeled back the double layer of foil and helped himself to a slice.

"Mmmph!" he commented with his mouth full and immediately grabbed another slice before reluctantly surrendering the loaf to me. "That is good stuff!"

Judy had apparently gotten out of bed in the wee hours to start the oven—a faint wisp of steam rose from the loaf as I peeled off the next slice, and I could feel the warmth where the foil rested on my thighs, even through eighteen ounces of wool and the long-handles. The bread itself melted on my tongue, the baked cranberries a counterpoint to the melted chocolate morsels with the tang of orange zest somewhere in the background. The poet Homer said that doves from earth "fly ambrosia home to father Zeus"—apparently, Judy had gotten that recipe.

"Should we save some for Wayne?" I asked nobody in particular as I stuffed another slice in my face.

"Nah," Ray said. "He's got his own loaf."

The bread was gone before we passed the first section road.

We stopped on the northeast corner of a quarter section of CRP with a waterway down one edge, choked with giant ragweed, and a scattering of redcedar on the hill. I walked with my shotgun in the crook of my left arm and my gloved hands in the game pocket of my vest. It was an awkward arrangement but had the one advantage of leaving some feeling in my fingers in the unlikely event that a bird might actually flush in gun range.

We were no more than a hundred yards from the vehicles with the dogs out ahead when Jim walked into a covey. I reacted to the sound of wings, fumbling to get my hands on the proper parts of the double gun, as eight or ten birds swept by me.

The thought flickered through my head: "Might as well take your time; they'll be gone before you get a shot off." With that encouraging notion in mind, I slowed down, picked out a cock bird, and swung through him before I hit the trigger. A puff of feathers, and he dropped into the edge of the ragweed. I was almost as surprised as he was.

The rest of the covey had disappeared through the ragweed, so I had little hope we would see them again. I folded myself back into the same awkward position to keep my hands warm. I hadn't gone another hundred yards when a single flushed to my left, flying back over my shoulder. An even tougher shot, with even less probability of success. I gathered the gun, turned, and dropped the bird just as he disappeared into the tall cover. By the time we got to the end of the waterway, I'd killed four wild-flushing bobwhite with four shots, a feat I'd never before accomplished and never expect to duplicate.

I was still marveling over the covey when we got to the south side of the CRP and turned west. Jim was on the edge where the grass met corn stubble when his shorthair pointed. He just had time to take his twenty gauge off his shoulder when a rooster flushed, twenty yards ahead. As the gun came up, I caught a second movement, farther out—a second rooster. Undistracted, Jim anchored the first bird, then swung to the second and folded it. Both stone dead. A true double on pheasants.

When we got back to the Suburban, I shook my head in amazement.

"That was some hour! After the last two days . . . Whatta you think changed?"

Jim allowed as how he couldn't tell but he was more than happy with developments.

Ray was quiet for a long minute.

"I wonder," he mused. "You don't suppose . . ." He paused again. "Maybe it was that bread."

The three of us stared at each other open-mouthed as the possibility sank in. Most days in the field are commonplace—long walks punctuated occasionally by a wild-flushing bird or a dog that takes it into his mind to go on walk-about, the sun following its arc low across the winter sky as the silent hours pass. But, now and then, there is a revelation, a moment when the answers to broader philosophical questions seem just at hand, insights into man's place in the universe, the meaning of life. The three of us were speechless as we contemplated the ramifications of this discovery.

We've encouraged Wayne, in the strongest possible terms, to seek patent protection for the list of ingredients and baking directions. He also needs to get Judy to give up her day job and start baking fulltime. He was receptive to the idea, especially when the rest of us volunteered to mortgage our homes to support the venture and Ray pointed out that it would entail no effort whatsoever on Wayne's part.

The stumbling block is Judy. She refuses to divulge the details of her bread-making, claiming it's a long-standing family secret. At first, she seemed willing to accept our offer as some sort of half-baked compliment; then, she regarded it as a bad joke. In the last couple of months, she's gotten more irritated when the idea is broached, threatening to change the locks on the house if any of us bring it up again.

So the biggest breakthrough in bird hunting since the discovery of gunpowder rests entirely on Wayne's aging shoulders. If he can get his hands on that recipe, we're in business. In the meantime, we're planning another Kansas rendezvous for next December. Jim and I are bringing the dogs and shells. Wayne's bringing the bread.

———————

A hard school

"TO ERR IS HUMAN; TO FORGIVE, DIVINE"—
the old verse came to me as I rolled down the high-
way in the dark, on the way home to a late supper.
We'd been hunting since dawn, the dogs and I, out of the
house in the wee hours of the morning to greet a frigid
gray dawn on a section of CRP cover that had held a few
pheasants over the first two months of the season. Then
on to the next. And the next. A long day, and, taken with
the previous day's exploits, remarkably discouraging.

I'd certainly lived up to the first half of the poet's
line, I thought. In less than forty-eight hours, I'd sinned
against nearly every precept in the pheasant hunter's
catalog of proper technique. As for the second half of
the line, if there is a divine presence that presides over
late-season pheasant hunting, it must be some member

of the Norse pantheon—Loki seems a likely possibility—
some god more inclined to torment a wandering hunter
for amusement than forgive his mistakes.

Young Finn the Brittany and I had started into the
cover half an hour before sunrise, as the first breeze
of the day whispered in from the northwest, cutting
through three layers of wool and nylon and making me
wish I'd brought my mittens. We walked the edge of the
grass along the corn stubble where a rooster should have
been feeding—no birds. No fresh tracks in the snow.

So we proceeded up the first draw to check the
kochia patches that were as close to shelter as a pheasant
could find on that weather-beaten patch of prairie. No
birds. Same with the second draw. And the third. We
worked our way back along the main ridge, checking the
head of every ravine, under the south-facing cutbanks
where the wind eased and the grass grew higher. No
birds.

Finally, after two hours of brush-busting and wind-
chill, we headed down the hill, back toward the truck.
One last spot—a check dam at the mouth of the last
draw. The switchgrass and little bluestem on the flanks
of the ravine gave way to a jungle of kochia in the bottom, already beaten down by several blizzards, now
waist-deep and almost impenetrable. Young Finn had
the good sense to go around the edge and sit on top of
the dam, watching as I waded through the thicket, which
seemed somehow backward, but I suppose one of us had
to do it.

I'd made it to the foot of the dam itself, a ten-foot
dike in the thickest of the kochia, when a rooster jumped
above me. It was a cagey maneuver, leaving me no more
than a fifteen-foot window of opportunity. I snapped the
shot at him just as he disappeared over the top, leaving

me wondering whether I'd done any damage or not. Then, a single flank feather floated down the wind and disappeared.

I have no mark on him, I thought. If he's crippled . . . I scrambled up the side of the dike, struggling to find footing, and got to the top to discover Finn standing over the bird with a matter-of-fact look on his face. Good dog.

We slid down the other side of the dam into the patch of kochia there, Finn disappearing into the brush as two hens flushed wild out the other side. He was out of the cover at the sound of the wings and in pursuit, in spite of my whistle. After a couple of useless tweets, I let him go, figuring he could use the lesson in futility.

The brush blended into the corner of a center-pivot cornfield, narrowing steadily to a sparse point out in the stubble. A rooster in the bag, I thought, and two hens—judging from the experience of the morning, this was more than I could legitimately expect from this patch. Fifteen-minute drive to the next covert. Maybe the truck will warm up enough to get some feeling back in my fingers.

And the second rooster flushed out of the last wisp of cover, a pathetic scrap that wouldn't have hidden a field mouse.

He was no more than twenty yards off my gun barrel. If I hadn't fumbled the safety, I'd probably have been alright, although the gun stuck on my right bicep as I mounted it, which complicated the shooting a little. Anyway, I missed. And missed again. He swung downwind and disappeared over the horizon as Finn appeared on the scene to join the excitement.

I checked my watch: 10:00 in the morning. Plenty of time, I thought, as I plodded toward the truck. But, seven hours later, as the light faded, those two roosters were the only ones we'd found.

The previous day had been, if anything, even worse. Freya, my veteran Britt, and I were working out another kochia draw. Eight hens and a rooster had flushed at 200 yards on the far end of the cover. She'd barked at them as they flew away, and, having registered her frustration with the opposition, she doubled back on the far slope into a stand of switchgrass and little bluestem. I followed, parallel to her and a hundred yards below, down to the other end of the ravine, which had produced birds on other hunts.

Two hundred yards down the draw, out of the wind and with the first morning sun giving the illusion of warmth on my back, I raised the ear flaps of my insulated cap and decided to get out of my shooting gloves as I walked. The right glove was halfway off when the rooster flushed, ten yards behind me. Pivoting 180 degrees to one's left while trying to pull off a glove and mount a shotgun is a complex maneuver. I didn't manage it. The gun butt never really got to my shoulder, and, as far as I can tell, I pulled the trigger with the ring finger of my right hand. It was not a good shot.

After I picked up my gloves and finished the stream of invective, I noticed Freya, near the top of the hill at the edge of a particularly dense patch of switch, as taut as the A string on a Stradivarius. I lumbered up the slope and was about fifty yards from her when the rooster tired of waiting and flushed out of range.

Two hours of hard walking later, she caught scent on the edge of a quarter section of CRP and trailed uphill. After my experience earlier in the day, I decided it might be a good idea to fall in behind her. She'd gone more than a hundred yards, quietly, carefully following the scent, when two hens and a pair of roosters flushed wild and disappeared over the top of the ridge. She wasn't inclined to give up on this bunch, and, since I had no better plan, I hiked up the slope and joined her on the ridgeline. A couple of hundred yards later, she pointed. A hen. Apparently, the birds had learned to fly out of sight, then tuck into the cover. Another point, another hen.

After she'd watched the second bird disappear, she looped out ahead and seemed to catch another scent. She worked her way across a saddle and up another slope on the far side as I watched, trying to decide whether it was worth following her. Finally, she was 200 yards out, a clear indication that the rooster she was trailing wasn't about to hold to a point. I blew the whistle to call her back . . . and, at the sound, a rooster flushed thirty yards to my right. As a right-handed shooter, I've always found it difficult to pivot to my right, especially when I've been ambushed. As the bird dove into the head of a nearby draw and gained speed, I saluted him with a single shot, just to confirm that my intentions were serious. He didn't seem at all impressed. Neither was Freya.

I've been hunting pheasants for nearly sixty years. In that time, I've been schooled by hard experience to observe all the pheasant-hunting commandments. I learned long ago that I should always be ready at the end of the cover. I know that, when a bird flushes, I should expect another one. That I should trust the dog. That, when I stop for any reason—to wait for the dog or another hunter, to take a breather, unzip my jacket, watch a flock of geese overhead, or to whistle the dog back—I should always be ready when I take the next step. I've recently become aware of one of the corollaries of these rules—don't try to take my gloves off while I'm walking a prime covert.

There's not much room for violations of the commandments in late-season pheasant hunting. The birds that have survived the autumn are immensely savvy, and there aren't all that many of them left. Where I hunt, there are about ten hours between sunrise and sunset at the end of the season, and, in that time, I may get three chances, if I'm lucky. Not three chances on pointed roosters flushing underfoot but three chances at birds that flushed thirty yards ahead of the dog or twenty yards behind me, birds that don't cackle as they rise and may not even slap a primary against a weed stem to let me know they've flown. Maybe three chances in ten hours, in twelve or fifteen miles of walking through heavy cover, through snow, often through weather no sane human would brave. When I miss one of those chances, it stings.

In such conditions, against such quarry, a hunter is bound to make mistakes. It's just that I would prefer to make new ones instead of repeating the old ones, over and over again. Apparently, that is not to be my lot. And so I take some solace in the poet's couplets:

"Ah, ne'er so dire a thirst for glory boast,

"Nor in the critic let the man be lost

"Good-nature and good sense must ever join;

"To err is human, to forgive, divine."

I suppose I have no choice but to accept the fact that, in spite of my best efforts to master the discipline of pheasant hunting, I'm bound to fall into error now and then. Maybe more often than now and then. That leaves the matter of forgiveness for my transgressions: I guess I'll have to grant that to myself. It seems the gods won't cut me any slack.

And I know the birds won't.

———

Last day

THE MONTH OF JANUARY WENT PRETTY MUCH the way I'd expected—more and more miles for fewer and fewer roosters. We were still seeing birds, Flick and I—fifty or sixty a day, sometimes—but as the month wound down, the average range of flushing birds steadily increased until, when Flick started working scent at my feet, I found myself watching the ridgeline for the flicker of wings. The GPS tally of the walks mounted steadily as the days passed: 12 miles, 13 miles, 14.8 miles, 15.2 miles of kochia and switchgrass and little bluestem, up and down the Nebraska hills from sunrise to sunset, hoping for one or two good chances. Hoping.

The last of the bird seasons closed at sunset on January 31, so, of course, Flick and I were on the road at four in the morning, the dog snoozing in a tight ball on the right seat while I navigated the black ice on the interstate in order to be in the cover at first light. We arrived to find six inches of fresh powder lying gently on the prairie grass, the stems bent in delicate arches over the roof of snow, draped with crystals they had gathered during the night, each one flashing as the sun touched it, the light shattered momentarily into the colors of the spectrum against the blue shadows.

It was a quarter of a mile from the road to the first patch of cover. I eased the truck door closed and started across the intervening corn stubble as quietly as I could, Flick at heel to minimize the chance of a wild flush. Ten minutes later at the northwestern corner of the grass, I released him with a wave of the hand, and he disappeared, leaving a trail of snow flakes suspended in the air above the switchgrass as he made his first swing.

We worked our way down the east slope of the ridge into the draw where the old International pickup body rusted slowly away in half an acre of kochia. For all our care, the birds knew we were coming. A rooster flushed wild sixty yards to my right, out of range on the far slope, followed by a second bird even farther away. Disappointment. I'd expected them, but I'd hoped the snow would convince them to hold a little longer. At the sound of the wings, Flick popped out of the grass thirty yards to my left and froze with his ears perked up and a look of disgust. I had to smile.

And, right then, the third rooster jumped, thirty yards away instead of sixty. I've played the game long enough now to keep the jolt of panic from an unexpected flush under some sort of control, but the urge to hurry was nearly overwhelming, as it always is. I shifted my feet as the Model 12 came to my shoulder, swung through the bird as he hit high gear, and pulled the trigger just an instant too early. He rocked but didn't fall. The second shot was longer but more considered. It caught him just as he rose to clear the cutbank on the other side of the cover, and he crumpled. Flick was there three seconds later to make sure he didn't run.

On the last day, one rooster in the bag is a major success, but it was early and, with the snow, there was reason to hope for more. We checked the patch of kochia at the corner of the field where we moved a lone hen who ran 200 yards before she flushed at the shoulder of the ridge and disappeared.

As I turned south, I saw another set of tracks heading out ahead in the first row of the corn stubble. Flick wasn't on the trail—yet—but I took the gun off my shoulder and quickened the pace. As I came over the next rise, he'd come out of the cover and was trotting down the field edge when a plume of scent grabbed him by the nose, spinning him ninety degrees as he pointed. I hurried to catch up, thinking that this was another hen— on the last day, roosters never hold to points.

But this one had. Flick was certain sure, as tight as a fiddle string, and I stepped in front of that unerring pink nose, reminding myself to relax, just as the rooster exploded out of the switchgrass in a cloud of snow, incandescent copper and green against a flawless morning sky, cackling as he went. He swung right, and, just as the muzzle of the gun caught up with him, banked back left. I managed to reprogram the change in trajectory, and he went down. Flick was there in a heartbeat to make sure he didn't run.

We worked another kochia covert that should have been loaded with birds, pushing one rooster out at more than eighty yards and crossing the tracks ten or fifteen birds had left as they melted into the wheat stubble to

the south. Then up the southern edge of the grass, a part
of the field that had never produced before. Halfway up
the slope, Flick pointed emphatically. I walked in, kicked
the cover, and turned to look at the dog. He moved three
steps and locked up again. I was doubtful—roosters
don't hold this way on the last day, especially on public
land. With the gun on my shoulder, I kicked half-heart-
edly at the tangle of grass in front of the dog . . . and a
rooster flushed, headed low over the cover to my left.

I've missed that shot on many occasions. But not this
time. He fell through the snow-covered canopy just short
of the fence, leaving a sparkling cloud of frost in the air.
And Flick was there to make sure of him.

As we walked the half-mile back to the truck, I found
myself puzzling over my feelings about the morning.

It had been almost perfect. The landscape, so often
cold and colorless at this time of year, had been trans-
formed in the middle of the night into a fairyland. With
the experience of another long season under his belt,
Flick had done his job about as well as it could be done,
instinct and training running straight and true in an
ancient channel, and after a season of out-maneuvering
and out-thinking hunter and dog, the birds had yielded,
at least for an hour or two. I'd even managed to do my
part with the wingshooting.

I've chased birds and dogs for more years than I care
to number, and if there's anything I've learned over that
time, it is that hunting well, with grace and honest effort,
respect and appreciation, is difficult, even for those of us
who have done it all our lives. What brings me back is
the pursuit of perfection.

But, in spite of the marvelous morning, I was more
than a little down in the mouth as I realized that this
was the last day. It'll be nine months before Flick and I

have another rendezvous with the birds. A long time to wait.

If the birds had all been wild; if the dog had run ahead and flushed the only rooster; if I had missed the one good chance, as I so often do; if the wind had swung into the north and pummeled us; if we had come back to the truck at sunset, footsore, chilled, and hungry with nothing to show for the effort except blisters and the questionable benefit of ten hours of hard walking—if, in short, it had been what the last day almost always is—then it might have been easier to let go. As it was, this hour had transcended the sum of its exquisite parts. Everything—the weather, the land, the light, the birds, the dog, even the hunter—had been close to some sort of unspoken ideal, and the combination was so fine that it brought a smile to my face and a tear to my eye. It's hard to let go of such days.

As I write this, Flick is sleeping in the corner, whining now and then, his feet twitching as he follows fresh scent through the coverts of his dreams. In this, as in so many other aspects of the hunt, he gives me an example to follow. Fall will come again. In the meantime, I'll take his lead and remember this day, savor it, until next November.

Evening———————

It's a white-hot existence. They live for two things—their people and the hunt. As the years go by, they learn the texture and scent of the untamed places we share with them, and they apply that expertise to the task at hand, slowing down, deciphering every nuance of behavior in their quarry, mastering an art that is mostly beyond our understanding. In their final years, the brilliance is almost palpable, a glow that surrounds the veterans as they stalk perfection. All too soon, the passion consumes them, and they leave their people behind to remember their lives and mourn their passing.

Closing time

WE CLOSED THE SEASON YESTERDAY, FREYA the Brittany and I, passing the last hours in a long walk over the hill to a place I call "the secret spot" because the best cover is out of sight from the road. We were both limping a bit, Freya because of the screw in her right elbow that holds the end of her humerus together but still gives her some arthritis, and I because an unexpected encounter with a badger hole a few miles back had given one of my aging knees a wrench.

Considering our condition, the prudent thing would have been to call it a day, but this was the last day, and I think it was fair to say that neither of us was willing give up the final hours. I knew it would be almost nine months before we passed this way again. Freya is probably not burdened with such foresight—the chase is simply her reason for being, the fire that courses through her veins and will not be stilled. So we went on to the bitter end.

Which brought us here, to the first day of February, with the northwest wind rattling the windows and threatening snow, bereft. Freya is curled up tightly in her favorite spot, recovering from the last hard week, her eyes following me as I walk in and out of the room, expecting another ride to the country. The vest is hanging in the closet; the boots are in the corner, their seams frayed, their toes polished black by the endless miles of prairie grass, thistle stems, and crop stubble, down at the heel, soles worn smooth. I have chores that have been too long postponed, but for this day at least, I'd rather look back over the last three months and consider what it was I found there.

There were birds, of course: neon rooster pheasants rising with a shower of frost in the first morning sun, coveys of bobwhite quail exploding underfoot, flocks of prairie chickens and sharptails beckoning on the horizon. We hunters speak of such moments in shorthand, stringing them together like jewels on a necklace, all too aware of just how rare and fleeting they are.

My overarching memory of the season is far less tangible. It is a feeling of sky and wind on my face; bright sun and snow squalls; cold that penetrated to the skin like an ice pick; sudden, unexpected warmth in the shelter of a cutbank; a short-eared owl floating over the grass; a prairie falcon streaking low over the cover like an arrow from the bow; fox tracks leading the way down the edge of the cover; crystals of frost clinging to the grass like diamonds in the dawn; a string of mule deer disappearing over the far ridge; the buck standing up, thirty yards away, in a stand of switchgrass; the fathomless indigo sky as the evening deepens and the stars emerge; a chevron of sandhill cranes bound for the Gulf of Mexico, their ancient traveling chant floating down out of heaven like an anthem. The fuzzy leaves of mullen flat to the ground, green in the depths of winter. The graceful curve of an empty milkweed pod. The drag of the heavy cover on my feet at the end of ten straight hours in the field. Knees that don't want to lift for the next step.

Such is the content of the hours and hours spent for the second of the shot. When I was young, I wanted one without the other. When the shooting was slow, I was irritated. Little by little, I learned what I was told was patience—distracting myself with thoughts of appointments, commitments, deadlines until the dog caught scent or I heard the slap of a primary on the grass behind me. I'm not sure that approach improved my wing shooting, but I suppose it lowered my blood pressure.

As the miles and the years have passed, I've settled into something altogether different. When I'm in the field, a thought will occasionally roll through my head, but mostly, I'm just there, behind the dog, in the moment. If I had to pick one word to describe the mental state, it would be meditation. The occasional points, the shots, the birds in the bag are a critical part of the whole—they supply the motivation for the day and test particular skills in hunter and dog.

But they aren't the only part.

After sixty years in the field, it seems that what I hunt is not only a bird, not only a day, but a frame of mind. Maybe even a state of grace. I can't tell where the importance of one stops and another starts. But I think it's why I keep coming back.

The rainbow

WE WERE HUNTING ON THE EDGE.
On the edge of a center pivot of corn stubble with corners of dense switchgrass and a shelter-belt of ponderosa pine along its northern boundary.

On the edge of a four-day span of Indian summer in the middle of December. The highs had been running in the low fifties, the clear solstice light filtering down between fair-weather clouds, the breeze in the southwest, hardly enough to stir the grass. But, on this morning, with the first sun of the day already warming behind us, there was a blue-black line across the horizon ahead with pearl-gray curtains of rain and snow suspended from the darkest murk. The sky confirmed what the weatherman had predicted—a dose of winter was headed our way.

On the edge of two lives:

One was Freya's, the apprentice, a month deep in her first real bird season. She was showing unmistakable signs of talent amid the frustrating lapses of attention and discipline that are a part of a young dog's development. She still had a lot to learn about the birds we were chasing, the cunning of the old ringnecks running ahead of her, the hair-trigger temperament of a covey of bob-white quail, the unpredictable ways of prairie grouse, sometimes holding to the point, more often flushing 200 yards away and disappearing over the horizon.

The other was Flick's. For eleven seasons, he'd been the rock on which every successful hunt was built—the unerring nose, the deep experience with every avian stratagem, the white-hot passion for the hunt. The arthritis in his hips had almost crippled him; his paws were knobby and warted with old injuries; his eyes were clouded with the sclerosis of advancing years. What sustained him was his unquenchable enthusiasm for the coverts and the birds, and so he came along on every trip, ready to contribute half an hour of perfect work in the morning and another at sunset, proving, once again, that the spirit can prevail, even when the flesh is weak.

Considering the approaching storm, I put both dogs down at once, loaded the gun, and set off through the first corner of the field. Flick quartered ten yards ahead while Freya worked back and forth through the switch-grass near the speed of sound, overrunning her nose, as a young dog will. She'd made her way half way across the patch when a sudden tendril of scent grabbed her by the nose and nearly broke her neck. Her back half skidded to a stop while her front half froze into a point, vibrating like a tuning fork.

I stopped Flick and walked up to see whether the pheasant had held in spite of Freya's lightning approach.

As I stepped in front of her nose, a hen flushed under my feet. I'd already turned to praise Freya for her work when the rooster followed. She nipped at his tail, and, after I got both feet back on the ground, I managed to remember to swing through him as he curved off to the right. Freya was on him before he bounced the second time. With the first bird in the back of the vest, I turned toward the cover on the lee side of the shelterbelt.

Flushed with success, Freya disappeared into the trees. Flick continued his methodical way down the edge of the grass as it narrowed, ten or twenty yards ahead, following his nose. He'd gone about a hundred yards when he turned into the wind and froze. No vibration, no forward lean—just the practiced point of a grizzled veteran. "Let the bird be there," I thought, as I caught up.

And he was. A young rooster, like molten copper in the morning sun, cackling in surprise at the sudden disturbance. I took him as he flattened out toward the trees and heard the thump as he hit the ground. As the gun came off my shoulder, there was a slap of primaries on the grass just behind. I swung around to see a second rooster curving out over the corn stubble. A rushed shot to no effect, and he disappeared over the rise as a third rooster flushed to my left. I stood with two empty shells in the gun and watched as he fled down the edge of the shelterbelt, the red of his flank glowing triumphantly against the pines, before he vanished around the corner.

Flick was standing over the first bird. It was his practice to retrieve the cripples and leave the dead birds to me, after he'd made sure they weren't going anywhere. I ran my hand down his flank before I picked up the bird—good dog, good dog.

In that moment, a gust of wind slammed down out of the north and a spatter of sleet rattled through the grass, still bright in the sunshine. I looked toward the storm clouds, now almost overhead—a rainbow spanned the northern horizon, the spectrum glowing against the darkness.

The high plains are rainbow country. In June when the thunderstorms mutter and grumble across the grass nearly every afternoon, there may be one a week. But, in nearly seventy years, this was the first one I'd ever seen in December.

I whistled for Freya and headed back to the truck. We had a long way to go, and there was a good chance the sleet would turn to snow before we made it home. As I walked, I considered the rainbow.

The physical explanation is straightforward enough, although, for me, the idea that uncounted trillions of raindrops could act in unison to create an immense projection against the sky has always seemed somehow supernatural. I've long harbored the suspicion that the old understanding was more accurate, that the rainbow was a sign from somewhere outside the world we understand. The Norsemen saw it as a bridge between this world and the next; the Old Testament says it's a signature, recognizing a covenant between the living things on earth and a forgiving God.

As it turned out, that pheasant was Flick's last. Two weeks later, I found him lying on the cold concrete floor of the basement, unable to get up. A visit to the vet confirmed my worst fears—the calcified arthritis in his spine and hips was finally bringing unbearable pressure to bear on critical nerves. He was in pain and could not stand. And so I asked for the last shot. As he slipped away, I whispered in his ear, through the tears: "Good dog. Good dog."

In the months since, I've often thought back to that

last point under the span of an impossible rainbow. I'm inclined to believe it was sent to Flick, an affirmation of a life lived in unwavering commitment to the discipline he had been born to follow. Or maybe little Freya shared in that moment of celestial recognition, the two of them on opposite ends of the great arc. Young and old. Promise and perfection.

Even now, I'm not sure. We hunters have been inclined toward superstition for as long as we've followed the chase, for longer than we've been human. It's possible that we should give up the old instincts—modern skepticism may be the only lens through which we should contemplate the world. But moments like these leave me wondering.

I know this for certain: From that day on the edge of things to the end of my days, whenever I see a rainbow, I'll think of Flick and all the other dogs I've known, and the birds, and, most of all, the wild places that have beckoned and whispered their secrets in my ear. May we all meet again . . . on the other end of the rainbow.

The bell

IT'S MADE OF BRASS, ABOUT THE DIAMETER OF a silver dollar with a nylon strap looped through the top so it can be strung on a collar. It has no markings, but the catalog house that sold it to me, many years ago, said it came from England—certainly, it has that English look and feel, an exquisite bit of craftsmanship from another time that combines simplicity, elegance, and dependability to do a job that is largely irrelevant in the modern age. It has a bright, clear tenor voice, not loud but surprisingly penetrating, even on a day when the first cold front of November is hurrying across the prairie, tousling the bluestem as it passes.

I must have bought it around 1987. I was starting Britt at the time. He was the most talented bird dog I've ever owned, and he was just starting to show his worth when we encountered the Conservation Reserve Program. We were used to working fencelines and shelterbelts, long strips of cover Britt could hunt from the outside. When he went on point, he was nearly always out in the stubble where I could see him. The bird might not hold, but there was at least no problem finding the dog.

The first CRP field we hunted was a full section of switchgrass just reaching maturity. Some of the seed heads were eight feet off the ground; the vegetation below was almost impenetrable. We both saw the potential and dived into the jungle with high expectations. I saw Britt's wake for the first fifty yards, then the grass was still. I stopped to listen for him. Not a whisper. I figured he was within sixty yards of me, almost certainly pointing a pheasant, and there was no way I was going to call him off that point.

I started a spiral search pattern, and in about five minutes, I found him, still holding, but with the relaxed tail that told me the scent had gone cold. The rooster had quietly departed for other hiding places.

By the time that field had finished with us, I could see that Britt and I needed some way of keeping track of each other if we intended to hunt any more CRP. The first generation of beeper collars had just been invented, but fresh out of college, I didn't have the money to buy one, and I didn't really want one anyway—inflicting that infernal beeping on the stillness of the day felt a little like spray-painting a mustache on the Mona Lisa. So I bought the bell.

We went back to that section of CRP on a clear, quiet morning with the temperature hovering around five. The frost lay like snow on the fields—I figured Britt would be able to smell a rooster from a quarter-mile away. He skirted the edge of the heavy grass for a hundred yards before a plume of scent lured him into the cover, and I listened as the bell traced his progress, out and across the lee of a low rise. Then, suddenly, nothing, a hole in the air where the clear *tink-tink* had been. I headed toward the last place I'd heard the sound, holding the shotgun high enough to keep the grass stems out of my eyes.

I almost stumbled over him, head high, stub tail at full attention, taut as a violin string. One more step and the rooster came straight up, clawing into the blue sky with a clatter and a squawk, his flanks incandescent in the first light.

Taken by surprise, as I nearly always am when a rooster flushes, I missed with the first shot but managed to catch him with the second. Britt disappeared into the switch, the bell marking his progress, farther away, farther, then a pause, closer, closer still, and suddenly, two amber eyes out of the wall of grass—Britt with the bird.

Over the next ten years, the two of us spent a lot of time in this strange, one-way telecommunication, Britt transmitting out of sight while I tried to interpret the message. I could tell a lot by the sound of the bell. There was a steady cadence with a syncopated flourish when he was quartering, looking for scent. When something caught his attention, the cadence broke, and the irregular notes of the bell signaled every move of his head. There was a Doppler change in the tone as he worked—higher as he came back toward me, lower as he went away. Early in his career, he was fond of pointing meadow voles, and I could often tell by the bell that his tail was wagging as he pointed, a sign that he was mousing. And now and then, that hole in the air, the sudden silence—a rooster, a covey, a band of chukars, a ruffed grouse, a blue, a bomber. We hunted them all, Britt following his unerring nose while I followed the bell.

One evening, the friend who had told me about Britt's litter called me about another litter in the same line, so on the way to a quail hunt in the Flint Hills, I stopped to look the pups over. That was how little Meg came to our house.

Britt tolerated her, and she paid him the respect due to his age and experience. They hunted together for two seasons before she inherited the bell. She might not have had the talent of her great uncle, but she was still a better bird dog than I deserve. I remember her pointing a pheasant on the slope of one of those huge prairie swales that break up the high plains, staunch in the wine-colored little bluestem as my partner walked in. The rooster flushed wild, and the shot rocked him but didn't break a wing. We watched and Meg watched as the bird flapped and glided, flapped and glided down the long slope, across the creek bed, and up the other side, almost to the horizon before he sat down.

My eyes dropped back to another movement, Meg crossing the creek bed on line. She trotted up the long slope on the far side, a tiny white speck by this time, paused on the hilltop, then turned back toward us. As she crossed the creek bed, I could see she was carrying something. She disappeared in the grass on our side, and a long minute passed before I heard the bell approaching. She walked up to me with the bird in her mouth. I took it and scratched her ear. Well done, little one.

The two of us chased many birds across many states to places I don't think I would ever have seen on my own: the pocket just under the rim of Tatman Mountain in northern Wyoming where a tiny spring waters a lush stand of wild rye and a perennial covey of Huns and you can see for fifty miles. The terrace in Iowa where there is always a rooster and Meg once pointed the biggest whitetail buck I've ever seen, caught napping in the switchgrass. The prairie slope above the Missouri River in North Dakota with its sharptails, the buffaloberries scarlet on the hillside and the hawthorn fruit fuschia against the gray branches in the draw.

The moments fade in the telling, like picked wildflowers, but in my memory they are forever bright against the background of the autumns we shared, the collection of days stitched together by the play of light and shadow on the grass, the sigh of the wind, and the tinkling of a small bell.

Not long after Meg passed her fourteenth birthday, a friend invited us to hunt his farm in western Iowa. The farm reflects Tom's commitment to conservation—terraces, grassy waterways, and buffer strips to keep the topsoil in place; blocks of conservation reserve to rebuild topsoil where it's been lost; and wetland reserve to purify the runoff. That kind of care produces pheasants even when the surrounding farms have been scalped for profit.

Meg was still good for two hours in the morning, and while her pace had slowed, her enthusiasm for the game was as bright as ever. On the morning of the fifth day, I was packing to leave, one bird short of Iowa's possession limit. Always the gracious host, Tom told me to stop and check one last hillside on my way to the interstate, so I headed south, Meg riding shotgun in the pickup, marking every meadowlark as it flushed off the side of the road.

The CRP Tom had recommended was a perfect corner for pheasants—bluestem and switchgrass with a mix of broad-leafed plants on a hillside just below a harvested cornfield. I unbuckled Meg's collar and slipped on the bell before I lifted her out of the truck, then grabbed the Model 12 and followed her down the fencerow. She disappeared into the grass, and I waited, listening to the bell as it made its invisible way down the slope. A hundred yards from the truck, it stopped.

I walked that way and found her just a couple of yards into the heavy cover, rock solid. As I passed her ear, two roosters exploded out of the grass. I picked the left bird and crumpled it. Meg disappeared. Then, I saw her coming back through the short brome of the field edge, tail and head up, with the rooster in her mouth, the light of the December morning warm on them both. A fine way to end a hunt, I thought, and a season.

At the time, I couldn't know that it was also the end of a career. That Iowa rooster was Meg's last bird.

And so the bell passed to Flick. He's eighteen months old now, with two seasons under his belt, a passion for rabbits, and a talent for birds. He's presided over the demise of about fifty pheasants already, and just last week, I had a chance to introduce him to some Kansas bobwhite. He didn't know what to make of the first covey, but he quickly filed the scent under the general heading of "game," trotted down the edge of the milo field to a thicket of sand plum and pointed a single. Which I promptly missed.

As I strolled along behind my new companion toward the next covert, it occurred to me that a bird hunter measures his life in dogs. With luck, I may have one more after Flick. Or he may be the last. Such thoughts can lead out into areas of metaphysics and theology I'm not qualified to navigate. Is there another world beyond the pale? I'm sure I don't know. But I find it hard to imagine a place much better than the one we were all born to, this small blue planet where life has gathered against all the odds.

I'm not anxious to leave. If I were given a choice between crossing over into an unknown paradise or melting back into the ground of this one, I think I'd just as soon stay. Still, there is the possibility that, when the time comes, the fields on the other side will be drenched in the rich morning sun of November with the scent of fall on the breeze . . . and the sound of a small brass bell, fading toward the horizon.

And, if that's the call, I just might have to follow.

Afterword:
About the killing

WE RENTED THE HOUSE FROM THE FARMER, whose wife had insisted some years before that they move to town. The place was ten miles east and a mile north of that cozy little Kansas settlement, up a dead-end road on the banks of a sand-bottomed creek with its border of scrub timber next to fields of bottomland alfalfa and corn, weedy fencerows and drainage ditches, and the abandoned rail line where the native prairie still grew. There were mallards and wood ducks on the creek, deer and wild turkeys along the banks, a burgeoning population of pheasants and two or three coveys of quail where the cover met the crops.

There have been a few times in my life when I could almost consider my pursuit of upland birds "subsistence hunting," which is to say that the expense of equipment, ammunition, clothing, and transportation was about the same as the cost of domestic fowl at the market. This was one of those times. In season, Lee the Brittany and I could leave the house an hour before sunset and be home in time for supper, often with a bird or two.

Alas, such living arrangements are vanishingly rare on the modern American landscape. After a few years of that rural idyll on the Great Plains, the job market led us to the suburbs of a much larger town, and the expense of upland bird hunting quickly overwhelmed the market value of the food it produced.

Surveys of public opinion have long shown that the average American grudgingly concedes a certain moral rectitude in hunting, as long as the justification is obtaining food. That same American is not comfortable with the act of killing itself—would never think of slaughtering a chicken, let alone butchering a steer—but is at least dimly aware of the fact that hamburgers and chicken nuggets don't grow on trees. Most Americans don't object too strenuously to my hunting if my primary motive is laying in a supply of meat.

Of course, there are elements of that subsistence approach to hunting besides the cost of obtaining wild protein. The birds the dogs and I bring home are not the genetically engineered, antibiotic-laden fowl that arrive at commercial meat counters in Styrofoam trays covered with plastic wrap. Wild birds may be more expensive than the domestic article, but they are a distillation of what's left of the wild on our modern landscapes, not the product of the Tyson laboratories and factory farms. They're also fine table fare.

Still, the ratio of pounds of meat procured to the cost of procuring it leads many thoughtful people to suspect that my primary reasons for pursuing upland birds have little to do with providing sustenance for my family. And, in this, at least, they would be right.

The truth is, meat isn't the main reason I hunt, particularly if the quarry is an upland bird. This is not subsistence hunting, and, while I cherish the birds in the kitchen and on the table, I have other, more compelling reasons for chasing them. For many Americans, this leads to the conclusion that my motives are frivolous at best and psychotic at worst. Animal rights activists are found of describing my time in the field as "killing for fun," and I must say that we hunters have done astonishingly little to rebut that characterization.

Hunters themselves often describe hunting in general, and upland bird hunting in particular, as a sport, a description that has long made me uncomfortable. For me, the term "sport" conjures visions of badminton and croquet, tennis, golf, slow-pitch softball. While I recognize that some of the practitioners of these pastimes take them very seriously—as I sometimes have myself—they're generally regarded as frivolous playtime, a footnote in human affairs of little real significance.

If there were no other distinction between hunting and "sport," the fact that a hunter will probably kill another living thing is more than enough to separate the two. The killing is not a trivial matter, and no hunter I respect treats it as such. But the climax of the hunt at the kill doesn't describe the totality of the experience any more than the climax of a novel describes the book.

The Spanish philosopher José Ortega y Gasset famously wrote that "one does not hunt to kill; rather, one kills in order to have hunted." On the surface, it seems a circular sort of reasoning, but it is an insight worth considering. It's become fashionable in some circles to talk about "hunting with a camera," as if getting a photograph of a game animal is the same thing as reducing it to possession. Ortega rightly objects to this sort of imitation of the genuine article:

"One can refuse to hunt," he writes, "but if one hunts one has to accept certain ultimate requirements without which the reality 'hunting' evaporates. The overpowering of the game, the tactile drama of its actual capture, and usually even more the tragedy of its death nurture the hunter's interest through anticipation and give liveliness and authenticity to all the previous work: the harsh confrontation with the animal's fierceness, the struggle with its energetic defense. . . . Without these ingredients the spirit of the hunt disappears. The animal's behavior is wholly inspired by the conviction that his life is at stake, and if it turns out that this is a complete fiction, that it is only a matter of taking his picture, the hunt becomes a farce and its specific tension evaporates. All of hunting becomes spectral when a photographic image, which is an apparition, is substituted for the prey."

A person with a pointing dog can do much the same thing as a wildlife photographer, going through the motions of the chase until the dog finds a bird, then flushing it and watching it fly away—a sort of "catch-and-release" hunt. This requires all the preparation of a real hunt—the training of the dog, the ability to recognize good ground, the willingness to take the time and make the effort to comb through the cover until the dog points. What it does not include is the zen-like art of wingshooting, the exquisite beauty of the bird in hand, the regret at having taken it, and, for the dog, the completion of an instinctive drive to catch and retrieve the quarry he has stalked. Importantly, it also fails to bring wild meat to the table, closing the circle between human and the untamed world that has produced the game. Getting a first-rate photograph of a game animal, watching the dog point during our summer walks, are rewarding experiences—I enjoy both—but Ortega is right: Without the kill, they are not hunting.

Ortega makes a careful distinction between simple killing and the act of hunting, emphasizing the knowledge of the quarry the hunter must have, the effort required in the chase, and, most of all, the balance that must be struck between the hunter's ability to take his quarry and the quarry's ability to escape. According to Ortega, these elements make the difference between hunting and mere slaughter.

I would add the simple ecological fact that all humans kill. Our mere presence on the planet means suffering and death for an untold number of living things, wild and domestic. The hunter—or, at least, any hunter worthy of the title—kills with full knowledge of his actions, with a recognition of his impact on the world, and with a commitment to sustaining thriving populations of the wild things he pursues.

In our day-to-day lives, humans kill in ignorance of all these things. This reality applies just about as much to the committed vegan as it does to the most avid consumer of spare ribs and buffalo wings, and it raises a critically important moral question: If killing is an unavoidable reality of life, is it better to kill with knowledge and a commitment to sustain wild populations or is it more ethical to simply ignore the lethal effect we have on other living things? Conscious recognition of the fact that we kill to survive seems not only the more defensible moral stance but also leads to the practical conclusion that we can't continue to have wildlife and wild places if we don't take active steps to support them. Killing with respect seems infinitely preferable to killing with indifference.

Besides these ethical insights, the chase has other lessons to impart. For me, hunting has become a form of meditation, a discipline that could properly be considered a martial art. Sooner or later, it requires strength, endurance, knowledge, skill, patience, and, above all, focus—the ability to invest oneself entirely in the moment for hours, even days, on end. It's a combination of virtues that can be almost impossible to achieve, even for an experienced hunter, a state of grace that, once experienced, draws many of us back to the field again and again.

This discipline has its ancillary benefits: The guilds of tree sparrows and juncos brightening a moment with call notes, like wind chimes in the kochia. The distant chorus of chevrons of geese far overhead on their way up and down a continent. The harrier floating over the grass, weightless on silent wings. The coyote, stopping at the top of the ridge to look over his shoulder before he disappears. The veil of a snow squall blurring the far horizon. The wine-rich color of little bluestem against the snow. The exquisite lapis blue of a flawless January sky over the prairie. The neon sunrises and sunsets on the Great Plains in the shortest months of the year. The bright shards of wildness tucked away on landscapes that have long been tamed. These are encounters not often granted to the casual visitor; they are reserved for the hunter.

And so, when I'm accused by some city-bound activist of "killing for fun," I can only say that, for me, hunting is "fun" in the same way that raising a family is fun, in the same way breathing is fun. These are spiritual matters, not easily understood and even harder to explain, especially to someone with whom I share no common experience or cultural frame. As my father used to say, trying to explain hunting to a nonhunter is like trying to explain sex to a eunuch.

Over many years, I've struggled to articulate these ideas, even to myself. I've come to think they might find a clearer, purer expression in our dogs than in their masters. Like us, they've hunted since before time began. The chase is bound up in their genes as it is in ours; it has shaped their bodies and spirits, their behavior and society, as it has ours.

As the season came to a close last year, Freya the Brittany and I were working downwind through a lush stand of switchgrass and bluestem. It was the last half hour of the day, the rich butterscotch light of the prairie sunset settling on the cover, giving an illusion of warmth as we worked our way back toward the truck and the long drive home. Freya swung wide in front of me, and, as she quartered up ahead, a plume of scent hit her like an electric shock. She swung into the wind and stood vibrating with the certainty of the invisible bird between us, the whisper of the evening breeze fading to silence as the tension rose between the two of them and made its way into my chest, the three of us acting on each other like magnets, attracted and repeled by invisible forces no science has yet defined. As I eased toward Freya and looked into that face, her amber eyes burned with a fire that echoes down from the beginning, the flame of all that that has ever been wild. What there is to be understood about the chase, I thought as I took the last step, is in those eyes.

———

Other thoughts on the matter

Ardrey, Robert, 1976. *The hunting hypothesis: A personal conclusion concerning the evolutionary nature of man*. Atheneum, New York, NY.

Askins, Charles, 1931. *Game bird shooting*. The MacMillan Company, New York, NY.

Babcock, Havilah, 1950. *My health is better in November*. University of South Carolina Press, Columbia, SC.

Bergström, Anders, et al., 2020. Origins and genetic legacy of prehistoric dogs. *Science* 370: 557-564.

Boschin, Francesco, et al., 2020. The first evidence for late Pleistocene dogs in Italy. *Scientific Reports* 10: 13313.

Chauvet, Jean-Marie, et al., 1996. *Dawn of art: The Chauvet Cave, the oldest known paintings in the world*. Harry N. Abrams, Inc., New York, NY.

Clutton-Brock, Juliet, 2012. *Animals as domesticates: A world view through history*. Michigan State University Press, Lansing, MI.

Conard, Nicholas J., et al., 2015. Excavations at Shoningen and paradigm shifts in human evolution. *Journal of Human Evolution* 89: 1-17.

Davis, Simon J.M., and François R. Valla, 1978. Evidence for domestication of the dog 12,000 years ago in the Natufian of Israel. *Nature* 276: 608-610.

Evans, George Bird, 1971. *The upland shooting life*. Alfred A. Knopf, New York, NY.

Evans, George Bird (ed.), 1979. *The upland gunner's book: An anthology*. The Amwell Press, Clinton, NJ.

Garcia, Michel-Alain, 2003. Ichnologie Générale de la grotte Chauvet. *Bulletin de la Société Préhistorique Française* 102(1): 103-108.

Germonpré, Mieje, et al., 2009. Fossil dogs and wolves from Paleolithic sites in Belgium, the Ukraine, and Russia: Osteometry, ancient DNA and stable isotopes. *Journal of Archaeological Science* 36: 473-490.

Grinnell, George Bird, 1910. *American game-bird shooting*. Forest & Stream Publishing, New York, NY.

Henriksen, Georg, 2010. *Hunters in the barrens: The Naskapi on the edge of the White Man's world*. Berhan Book, New York, NY.

Hill, Gene, 1972. *A hunter's fireside book: Tales of dogs, ducks, birds and guns*. Winchester Press, New York NY.

Hill, Kim, 1982. Hunting and human evolution. *Journal of Human Evolution* 11(6): 521-544.

Holland, Ray, 1929. *My gun dogs*. Houghton Mifflin Company, New York, NY.

Holland, Ray, 1961. *Seven grand gun dogs*. Thomas Nelson & Sons, New York, NY.

Kurtén, Björn, 2009. *Pleistocene mammals of Europe*. Aldine Transaction, Aldine Publishing Company, Chicago, IL.

Lee, Richard B., and Irven DeVore, 1968. *Man the hunter*. Aldine De Gruyter, Hawthorne, NY.

Leopold, Aldo, 1953. *The round river*. Oxford University Press, New York, NY.

Lopez, Barry, 1978. *Of wolves and men*. Charles Scribner's Sons, New York, NY.

Madson, John, 1962. *The ring-necked pheasant*. Conservation Department, Olin Mathieson Chemical Corp., East Alton, IL.

Madson, John, 1979. *Out home*. Winchester Press, New York, NY.

McHugo, Gillian P., et al., 2019. Unlocking the origins and biology of domestic animals using ancient DNA and paleogenomics. *BMC Biology* 17: 98.

Ortega y Gasset, José, 1972. *Meditations on hunting*. Charles Scribner's Sons, New York, NY.

Ovodov, Nikolai D., et al., 2011. A 33,000-year-old incipient dog from the Altai Mountain of Siberia: Evidence of the earliest domestication disrupted by the last glacial maximum. *PLoS ONE* 6(7).

Perri, Angela R., et al., 2020. Dog domestication and the dual dispersal of people and dogs into the Americas. *Proceedings of the National Academies of Science* 118(6).

Posewitz, Jim, 1994. *Beyond fair chase*. Falcon Publishing, Globe Pequot Press, Guilford, CT.

Posewitz, Jim, 1999. *Inherit the hunt*. Falcon Publishing, Inc., Helena, MT.

Posewitz, Jim, 2004. *Rifle in hand: How wild America was saved*. Riverbend Publishing, Helena, MT.

Reiger, George, 2001. *American sportsmen and the origins of conservation*. Oregon State University Press, Corvallis, OR.

Roach, Neil T., 2013. Elastic energy storage and the evolution of high-speed throwing in *Homo*. *Nature* 498: 483-486.

Ruark, Robert, 1957. *The old man and the boy*. Henry Holt and Company, Inc., New York, NY.

Serpell, James, 2017. *The domestic dog: Its evolution, behavior and interactions with people*. Cambridge University Press, Cambridge, UK.

Shea, John J., and Matthew L. Sisk, 2010. Complex projectile technology and *Homo sapiens* dispersal into western Eurasia. *Paleoanthropology* 2010: 100-122.

Spiller, Burton L., 1962. *Drummer in the woods*. D. Van Nostrand Company, Princeton, NJ.

Stephanson, Robert, and B. Ahgook, 1975. The Eskimo hunter's view of wolf ecology and behavior, pp. 286-291, in Fox, M.W., *The wild canids: Their systematics, behavioral ecology and evolution*. Van Nostrand Reinhold Company, New York, NY.

Thieme, Harmut, 1997. Lower Paleolithic hunting spears from Germany. *Nature* 385: 807-810.

Valdene, Guy de la, 2011. *The fragrance of grass*. Lyons Press, Guilford, CT.

Vidal, Céline M., et al., 2022. Age of oldest known *Homo sapiens* from eastern Africa. *Nature* 601: 579-583.

Vilà, Carles, et al., 1997. Multiple and ancient origins of the domestic dog. *Science* 276: 1687-1689.

Wang, Guo-dong, et al., 2013. The genomics of selection in dogs and the parallel evolution between dogs and humans. *Nature Communications* 4: 1860; DOI: 10.1038.

Williams, Ben O., 2001. *Hunting the quails of North America*. Willow Creek Press, Minocqua, WI.

About the author

Born in Ames, Iowa, Chris Madson received a bachelor's degree in biology at Grinnell College and a master of science degree in wildlife ecology at the University of Wisconsin-Madison before accepting the editorship of *Kansas Wildlife* magazine in 1978 with what was then the Kansas Fish and Game Commission.

In 1983, he moved to Cheyenne to take the editorship of *Wyoming Wildlife* magazine for the Wyoming Game and Fish Department, a position he held until he retired in 2014. In that period, *Wyoming Wildlife* won more than 200 national awards for excellence in writing, photography, and design.

Madson has written for many other publications, including *Audubon, Outdoor Life, National Wildlife, Ducks Unlimited, Sporting Classics*, and *Pheasants Forever*. In 2005, Ducks Unlimited recognized him as its national Conservation Communicator of the Year, and in 2010, the National Wildlife Federation honored him with its National Conservation Achievement Award. In 2014, the University of Wyoming's Berry Biodiversity Institute recognized Madson's work with its first annual Contributions to Wyoming Biodiversity Conservation Award.

There isn't much in the outdoors he doesn't like to do—fishing, birding, landscape photography, canoeing, backpacking, and hiking. For the last forty years, his family's primary sources of meat have been wild—elk, deer, antelope, ducks and geese . . . and, of course, upland birds.